TypeScript 2.x for Angu.... Developers

Harness the capabilities of TypeScript to build cutting-edge web apps with Angular

Christian Nwamba

Pack<t>

BIRMINGHAM - MUMBAI

TypeScript 2.x for Angular Developers

First published: December 2017

Production reference: 1051217

Published by Packt Publishing Ltd.
Livery Place
35 Livery Street
Birmingham
B3 2PB, UK.
ISBN: 978-1-78646-055-4

www.packtpub.com

Credits

Authors
Christian Nwamba

Reviewers
Andrew Macrae

Commissioning Editor
Merint Mathew

Acquisition Editor
Reshma Raman

Content Development Editor
Nikhil Borkar

Technical Editor
Jash Bavishi

Copy Editor
Muktikant Garimella

Project Coordinator
Ulhas Kambali

Proofreader
Safis Editing

Indexer
Francy Puthiry

Graphics
Jason Monteiro

Production Coordinator
Shantanu Zagade

About the Author

Christian Nwamba is a Lagos, Nigeria-based full stack engineer, developer, and evangelist. He spends most of his life building user experiences with JavaScript and spreading the word to other developers through conferences, meetups, and technical articles.

He has worked with quite a few interesting SaaS companies, such as Cloudinary, Pusher, and Auth0, and has published articles on popular blogs, such as Sitepoint, Scotch.io, Codementor, and Web Designer Depot. This is his first book and he's very proud of the effort he put in to make it enjoyable for the readers.

He has a lot of interest in community building and efforts, especially in Africa. He does this by organizing and facilitating meetups/conferences (forLoop Africa, Angular Nigiera, GDGs, and more).

Acknowledgments

Before anything, I would like to express my sincere gratitude to my parents, Edwin Nwamba and Helen Nwamba, for nurturing and playing a huge role in my literary and technical upbringing. Their guidance gave me a great head start, which made all this possible.

Besides my parents, I would also like to thank the Scotch, Cloudinary, and Packt teams for the continuous and unrestrained support they showed to me during my time writing this book. I couldn't have asked for a better support in all sincerity.

My sincere thanks also go to Chris Sevilleja, Nick Cerminara, and Prosper Otemuyiwa for challenging me to become even better at what I do and for their encouragement, insightful comments, and hard questions. Also, I thank Marcel Nwamadi and Olayinka Omole for contributing to the technical success of this work.

I would like to thank Angular Nigeria and ForLoop Africa, two communities whose growth in recent times spurred me to carry on and not to relent in my efforts to make programming the mainstay in Africa.

I thank my friends, William Imoh, Raphael Ugwu, Nnaemeka Ogbonnaya, and Chioma Imoh, for the stimulating discussions, the constant reminders and evaluations, and for being with me in good times and bad through the last five years.

Last but not least, I would like to thank my siblings, Kelechi Nwamba, Ezinne Nwamba, Ekoma Nwamba, and Chioma Nwamba, for supporting me throughout my life.

About the Reviewer

Andrew Leith Macrae first cut his programming teeth on an Apple IIe, poking bytes into the RAM. Over the years, he has developed interactive applications with Hypercard, Director, Flash, and more recently, Adobe AIR for mobile. He has also worked with HTML since there was HTML to work with and is currently working as a senior frontend developer at The Learning Channel (`www.tsc.ca`), using Angular 4 with TypeScript. He is convinced that TypeScript is the future of JavaScript, bringing the structure and discipline of strongly typed object-oriented language to facilitate efficient, intentional coding for the development of large-scale applications for the web.

You can find out more about Andrew or contact him at `www.adventmedia.net`.

www.PacktPub.com

For support files and downloads related to your book, please visit www.PacktPub.com.

Did you know that Packt offers eBook versions of every book published, with PDF and ePub files available? You can upgrade to the eBook version at www.PacktPub.com and as a print book customer, you are entitled to a discount on the eBook copy. Get in touch with us at service@packtpub.com for more details.

At www.PacktPub.com, you can also read a collection of free technical articles, sign up for a range of free newsletters and receive exclusive discounts and offers on Packt books and eBooks.

Mapt

https://www.packtpub.com/mapt

Get the most in-demand software skills with Mapt. Mapt gives you full access to all Packt books and video courses, as well as industry-leading tools to help you plan your personal development and advance your career.

Why subscribe?

- Fully searchable across every book published by Packt
- Copy and paste, print, and bookmark content
- On demand and accessible via a web browser

Customer Feedback

Thanks for purchasing this Packt book. At Packt, quality is at the heart of our editorial process. To help us improve, please leave us an honest review on this book's Amazon page at https://www.amazon.com/dp/1787286436.

If you'd like to join our team of regular reviewers, you can email us at customerreviews@packtpub.com. We award our regular reviewers with free eBooks and videos in exchange for their valuable feedback. Help us be relentless in improving our products!

Table of Contents

Preface

Deciding to learn Angular can be quite overwhelming. This is because the de facto way of writing an Angular app is by using a superset language, TypeScript, which is fairly new. Ironically, TypeScript simplifies how Angular apps are written by providing strict types (as seen in strictly typed languages such as Java), which improves the predictive behavior of the apps we write. This book is intended to assist you as a beginner/intermediate Angular developer with little or no knowledge of TypeScript or strict typing, in general, by explaining the core concepts of TypeScript.

What this book covers

Chapter 1, *From Loose Types to Strict Types*, discusses the problems developers faced before TypeScript was introduced, and what problems TypeScript solves. We will do this by discussing loose types and their challenges, and show some examples of how these challenges were being tackled previously and why TypeScript is a better choice.

Chapter 2, *Getting Started with Typescript*, gives a summary of TypeScript's core concepts with practical examples on how to set up a vanilla JavaScript plus TypeScript project. All loosely typed examples in Chapter 1, *From Loose Types to Strict Types*, will be rewritten with TypeScript to demonstrate TypeScript's efficiency.

Chapter 3, *Typescript Native Types and Features*, takes a deep dive into built-in TypeScript strict types that match existing JavaScript loose types. Each type will be discussed extensively with working examples, showing how it should be used and how it should work.

Chapter 4, *Up and Running with Angular and TypeScript*, discusses how TypeScript applies to Angular. To do so, Angular needs to be up and running with the help of the CLI tool. In this chapter, we will discuss what it takes to have Angular and TypeScript work together. We will also cover the basic Angular concepts that you could find in a *Hello World* example.

Chapter 5, *Advanced Custom Components with TypeScript*, discusses the concept of web components and how Angular builds on web components with TypeScript. We will see how to create components with classes, implement lifecycle hooks with TypeScript interfaces, and define components, metadetails using TypeScript decorators.

Chapter 6, *Component Composition with TypeScript*, discusses how Angular is component-based. It explains that components are composed together as building blocks to make a fully functional app. We will discuss modularizing components using composition with examples and component interaction (data transfer and events). In doing so, we will see how TypeScript is used to keep us in check with all these moving parts.

Chapter 7, *Separating Concerns with Typed Services*, discusses how it's bad practice to allow our logic to live in our components. In such a case, Angular allows you to provide API methods via services that these components can consume. We will discuss how TypeScript helps us create contracts (using types) between these API methods and the components.

Chapter 8, *Better Forms and Event Handling with TypeScript*, explains how the Angular form module enables us to write predictable typed forms with TypeScript, which is a perfect means of collecting data from our app users. We will also see how to use typed DOM events (for example, click, mouseover, and keydown) to respond to user interactions.

Chapter 9, *Writing Modules, Directives, and Pipes with TypeScript*, discusses the secondary building blocks of Angular and how they are best used with TypeScript. You will learn how to build custom directives and pipes in Angular with types and decorators.

Chapter 10, *Client-Side Routing for SPA*, explains Single Page Applications (SPAs), which are built by handing over routing to the client with JavaScript rather than the server. We will discuss how, with Angular and TypeScript, we can use the router module to build multiple view apps with just a single server route.

Chapter 11, *Working with Real Hosted Data*, takes a deep dive into consuming API data with Angular's HTTP module. You will learn how to make an HTTP request right from our Angular app. Data fetched from this request can then be rendered by components.

Chapter 12, *Testing and Debugging*, covers recommended practices on unit testing Angular building blocks. These include components, services, routes, and more.

What you need for this book

The examples covered in this book can be implemented on a Windows, Linux, or macOS PC. You'll need to install Node and npm to work with TypeScript, and a decent web browser.

Who this book is for

This book is intended to assist a beginner/intermediate Angular developer with little or no knowledge about TypeScript or strict typing, in general, by explaining the core concepts of TypeScript. It's also a perfect book for developers who have already worked with Angular 1.x or other frameworks and are trying to move to Angular 2.x.

Conventions

In this book, you will find a number of text styles that distinguish between different kinds of information. Here are some examples of these styles and an explanation of their meaning.

Code words in text, database table names, folder names, filenames, file extensions, pathnames, dummy URLs, user input, and Twitter handles are shown as follows: "We can include other contexts through the use of the `include` directive."

A block of code is set as follows:

```
[default]
exten => s,1,Dial(Zap/1|30)
exten => s,2,Voicemail(u100)
exten => s,102,Voicemail(b100)
exten => i,1,Voicemail(s0)
```

When we wish to draw your attention to a particular part of a code block, the relevant lines or items are set in bold:

```
[default]
exten => s,1,Dial(Zap/1|30)
exten => s,2,Voicemail(u100)
exten => s,102,Voicemail(b100)
exten => i,1,Voicemail(s0)
```

Any command-line input or output is written as follows:

```
# cp /usr/src/asterisk-addons/configs/cdr_mysql.conf.sample
/etc/asterisk/cdr_mysql.conf
```

New terms and **important words** are shown in bold. Words that you see on the screen, for example, in menus or dialog boxes, appear in the text like this: "Clicking the **Next** button moves you to the next screen."

Warnings or important notes appear in a box like this.

Tips and tricks appear like this.

Reader feedback

Feedback from our readers is always welcome. Let us know what you think about this book—what you liked or disliked. Reader feedback is important for us as it helps us develop titles that you will really get the most out of.

To send us general feedback, simply e-mail feedback@packtpub.com, and mention the book's title in the subject of your message.

If there is a topic that you have expertise in and you are interested in either writing or contributing to a book, see our author guide at www.packtpub.com/authors.

Customer support

Now that you are the proud owner of a Packt book, we have a number of things to help you to get the most from your purchase.

Downloading the example code

You can download the example code files for this book from your account at http://www.packtpub.com. If you purchased this book elsewhere, you can visit http://www.packtpub.com/support and register to have the files emailed directly to you. You can download the code files by following these steps:

1. Log in or register to our website using your email address and password.
2. Hover the mouse pointer on the **SUPPORT** tab at the top.
3. Click on **Code Downloads & Errata**.
4. Enter the name of the book in the **Search** box.

5. Select the book for which you're looking to download the code files.
6. Choose from the drop-down menu where you purchased this book from.
7. Click on **Code Download**.

Once the file is downloaded, please make sure that you unzip or extract the folder using the latest version of:

- WinRAR / 7-Zip for Windows
- Zipeg / iZip / UnRarX for Mac
- 7-Zip / PeaZip for Linux

The code bundle for the book is also hosted on GitHub at
`https://github.com/PacktPublishing/TypeScript-2.x-for-Angular-Developers`. We also have other code bundles from our rich catalog of books and videos available at `https://github.com/PacktPublishing/`. Check them out!

Downloading the color images of this book

We also provide you with a PDF file that has color images of the screenshots/diagrams used in this book. The color images will help you better understand the changes in the output. You can download this file from `https://www.packtpub.com/sites/default/files/downloads/TypeScript2.xforAngularDevelopers_ColorImages.pdf`.

Errata

Although we have taken every care to ensure the accuracy of our content, mistakes do happen. If you find a mistake in one of our books-maybe a mistake in the text or the code-we would be grateful if you could report this to us. By doing so, you can save other readers from frustration and help us improve subsequent versions of this book. If you find any errata, please report them by visiting `http://www.packtpub.com/submit-errata`, selecting your book, clicking on the **Errata Submission Form** link, and entering the details of your errata. Once your errata are verified, your submission will be accepted and the errata will be uploaded to our website or added to any list of existing errata under the Errata section of that title. To view the previously submitted errata, go to `https://www.packtpub.com/books/content/support` and enter the name of the book in the search field. The required information will appear under the **Errata** section.

Piracy

Piracy of copyrighted material on the internet is an ongoing problem across all media. At Packt, we take the protection of our copyright and licenses very seriously. If you come across any illegal copies of our works in any form on the internet, please provide us with the location address or website name immediately so that we can pursue a remedy. Please contact us at copyright@packtpub.com with a link to the suspected pirated material. We appreciate your help in protecting our authors and our ability to bring you valuable content.

Questions

If you have a problem with any aspect of this book, you can contact us at questions@packtpub.com, and we will do our best to address the problem.

1
From Loose Types to Strict Types

JavaScript is loosely typed. It's worth repeating, *JavaScript is loosely typed.* Notice how the sentence is passive--we cannot categorically hold someone responsible for the loose-type nature of JavaScript just as we can't do so for other famous glitches of JavaScript.

A detailed discussion on what loose-types and loosely typed languages are will help aid your understanding of the problem that we plan to solve with this book.

When a programming language is loosely typed, it means that the data passed around using variables, functions, or whatever member applicable to the language does *not* have a defined type. A variable x could be declared, but the kind of data it holds is never certain. Loosely typed languages are contrary to strongly typed languages, which enforce that every declared member must strictly define what sort of data it can hold.

These types are categorized into:

- Strings
- Numbers (int, float, and so on.)
- Data structures (arrays, lists, objects, maps, and so on.)
- Boolean (true and false)

JavaScript, PHP, Perl, Ruby, and so on, are all examples of loosely typed languages. Java, C, C#, are examples of strongly typed languages.

In loosely typed languages, a member may be initially defined as a string. Down the line, this member could end up storing a number, a boolean, or even a data structure. This instability leads us to the implications of loosely typed languages.

Term definitions

Before we keep moving, it would be nice to define the common jargon you may have met or will meet with in the course of understanding loose and strict types:

- **Members**: These are the features of a language that describe how the data is stored and manipulated. Variables, functions, properties, classes, interfaces, and so on, are all examples of the possible members a language can have.
- **Declared versus defined versus assigned**: When a variable is initialized with no value, it is said to be *declared*. When it is declared and has a type, it is said to be *defined*. When the variable has a value, whether typed or not, it is *assigned*.
- **Types**: These are used to categorize the data based on how they are parsed and manipulated. For example, numbers, strings, booleans, arrays, and so on.
- **Values**: The data assigned to a given member is known as the member's value.

Implications of loose types

Let's start out with an example to show how loosely typed languages behave:

```
// Code 1.1

// Declare a variable and assign a value
var x = "Hello";

// Down the line
// you might have forgotten
// about the original value of x
//
//
// Re-assign the value
x = 1;

// Log value
console.log(x); // 1
```

The variable x was initially declared and assigned a string value, Hello. The same x got re-assigned to a numeric value, 1. Nothing went wrong; the code was interpreted and when we logged the value to the console, it logged the latest value of x, which is 1.

This is not just a string-number thing; the same thing applies to every other type, including complex data structures:

```
// Code 1.2

var isCompleted;

// Assign null
isCompleted = null;
console.log('When null:', isCompleted);

// Re-assign a boolean
isCompleted = false;
console.log('When boolean:', isCompleted);

// Re-assign a string
isCompleted = 'Not Yet!';
console.log('When string:', isCompleted);

// Re-assign a number
isCompleted = 0;
console.log('When number:', isCompleted);

// Re-assign an array
isCompleted = [false, true, 0];
console.log('When array:', isCompleted);

// Re-assign an object
isCompleted = {status: true, done: "no"};
console.log('When object:', isCompleted);

/**
 * CONSOLE:
 *
 * When null: null
 * When boolean: false
 * When string: Not Yet!
 * When number: 0
 * When array: [ false, true, 0 ]
 * When object: { status: true, done: 'no' }
 */
```

The important thing to note here is not that the *values* are changing. Rather, it's the fact that both values and *types* are changing. The change in the type does not affect the execution. Everything works fine, and we have our expected result in the console.

The function parameters and return types are not left out either. You can have a function signature that accepts a string parameter, but JavaScript will keep silent when you, or any other developer, pass in a number while calling the function:

```
function greetUser( username ) {
 return `Hi, ${username}`
}

console.log('Greet a user string: ', greetUser('Codebeast'))
console.log('Greet a boolean: ', greetUser(true))
console.log('Greet a number: ', greetUser(1))

/**
 * CONSOLE:
 *
 * Greet a user string: Hi, Codebeast
 * Greet a boolean: Hi, true
 * Greet a number: Hi, 1
 */
```

If you're coming from a strong-type background and have no previous experience with loosely typed languages, the preceding example must feel weird. This is because in strongly typed languages, it's hard to change the type of the particular member (variables, functions, and so on).

So, what is the implication to take note of? The obvious implication is that the members that are loosely typed are inconsistent. Therefore, their value types can change, and this is something that you, the developer, will need to watch out for. There are challenges in doing so; let's talk about them.

The problem

Loose types are tricky. At first glance, they appear to be all nice and flexible to work with-- flexibility, as in giving you the freedom to change types anytime and anywhere, without the interpreter screaming errors like other strongly typed languages do. Just like any other form of freedom, this one also comes with a price.

The major problem is inconsistency. It is very easy to forget the original type for a member. This could lead you to handling, say, a string as if it were still a string when its value is now Boolean. Let's see an example:

```
function greetUser( username ) {
  // Reverse the username
  var reversed = username.split('').reverse().join('');
  return `Hi, ${reversed}`
}

console.log('Greet a correct user: ', greetUser('Codebeast'))


  * CONSOLE:
  *
  * Greet a correct user: Hi, tsaebedoC
  */
```

In the preceding example, we have a function that greets the users based on their usernames. Before it does the greeting, it first reverses the username. We can call the function by passing in a username string.

What happens when we pass in a Boolean or some other type that does not have a `split` method? Let's check it out:

```
// Code 1.4

function greetUser( username ) {
  var reversed = username.split('').reverse().join('');
  return `Hi, ${reversed}`
}

console.log('Greet a correct user: ', greetUser('Codebeast'))

// Pass in a value that doesn't support
// the split method
console.log('Greet a boolean: ',greetUser(true))


  * CONSOLE:
  *
  * Greet a correct user: Hi, tsaebedoC
  * /$Path/Examples/chapter1/1.4.js:2
  * var reversed = username.split('').reverse().join('');
                            ^
  * TypeError: username.split is not a function
  */
```

The first log output, which prints the greeting with a string, comes out fine. But the second attempt fails because we passed in a Boolean. In as much as *everything* in JavaScript is an object, a Boolean does not have a `split` method. The image ahead shows a clear output of the preceding example:

```
● ● ●                          Chapter1 — -bash — 80×24
Last login: Tue May 30 14:36:23 on ttys001
Chriss-MacBook-Pro:Chapter1 chrisnwamba$ node 1.4.js
Greet a correct user:  Hi, tsaebedoC
/Users/chrisnwamba/Projects/Books/TS for Angular Devs/Examples/Chapter1/1.4.js:2
    var reversed = username.split('').reverse().join('');
                            ^

TypeError: username.split is not a function
    at greetUser (/Users/chrisnwamba/Projects/Books/TS for Angular Devs/Examples
/Chapter1/1.4.js:2:29)
    at Object.<anonymous> (/Users/chrisnwamba/Projects/Books/TS for Angular Devs
/Examples/Chapter1/1.4.js:7:33)
    at Module._compile (module.js:571:32)
    at Object.Module._extensions..js (module.js:580:10)
    at Module.load (module.js:488:32)
    at tryModuleLoad (module.js:447:12)
    at Function.Module._load (module.js:439:3)
    at Module.runMain (module.js:605:10)
    at run (bootstrap_node.js:420:7)
    at startup (bootstrap_node.js:139:9)
Chriss-MacBook-Pro:Chapter1 chrisnwamba$
```

Yes, you might be thinking that you're the author of this code; why would you pass in a Boolean when you designed the function to receive a string? Remember that a majority of the code that we write in our lifetime is not maintained by us, but by our colleagues.

When another developer picks up greetUser and decides to use the function as an API without digging the code's source or documentation, there is a high possibility that he/she won't pass in the right value type. This is because *he/she is blind*. Nothing tells him/her what is right and what is not. Even the name of the function is not obvious enough to make her pass in a string.

JavaScript evolved. This evolution was not just experienced internally but was also seen in its vast community. The community came up with best practices on tackling the challenges of the loose-type nature of JavaScript.

Mitigating loose-type problems

JavaScript does not have any native obvious solution to the problems that loose types bring to the table. Rather, we can use all forms of manual checks using JavaScript's conditions to see whether the value in question is still of the intended type.

We are going to have a look at some examples where manual checks are applied in order to retain the integrity of the value types.

The popular saying that *Everything is an Object* in JavaScript is not entirely true (https://blog.simpleblend.net/is-everything-in-javascript-an-object/). There are *Objects* and there are *Primitives*. Strings, numbers, Boolean, null, undefined, are primitives but are handled as objects only during computation. That's why you can call something like .trim() on a string. Objects, arrays, dates, and regular expressions are valid objects. It's mind-troubling to say that an object is an object, but that is JavaScript for you.

The typeof operator

The typeof operator is used to check the type of a given operand. You can use the operator to control the harm of loose types. Let's see some examples:

```
// Code 1.5
function greetUser( username ) {
  if(typeof username !== 'string') {
    throw new Error('Invalid type passed');
  };
  var reversed = username.split('').reverse().join('');
  return `Hi, ${reversed}`
```

```
  }

  console.log('Greet a correct user: ', greetUser('Codebeast'))
  console.log('Greet a boolean: ',greetUser(true))
```

Rather than waiting for the system to tell us that we're wrong when an invalid type is passed in, we catch the error as early as possible and throw a custom and more friendly error, as shown in the following screenshot:

```
● ● ●                      Chapter1 — -bash — 80×24
Chriss-MacBook-Pro:Chapter1 chrisnwamba$ node 1.5.js
Greet a correct user:  Hi, tsaebedoC
/Users/chrisnwamba/Projects/Books/TS for Angular Devs/Examples/Chapter1/1.5.js:3
      throw new Error('Invalid type passed');
      ^

Error: Invalid type passed
    at greetUser (/Users/chrisnwamba/Projects/Books/TS for Angular Devs/Examples
/Chapter1/1.5.js:3:13)
    at Object.<anonymous> (/Users/chrisnwamba/Projects/Books/TS for Angular Devs
/Examples/Chapter1/1.5.js:10:33)
    at Module._compile (module.js:571:32)
    at Object.Module._extensions..js (module.js:580:10)
    at Module.load (module.js:488:32)
    at tryModuleLoad (module.js:447:12)
    at Function.Module._load (module.js:439:3)
    at Module.runMain (module.js:605:10)
    at run (bootstrap_node.js:420:7)
    at startup (bootstrap_node.js:139:9)
Chriss-MacBook-Pro:Chapter1 chrisnwamba$
```

The `typeof` operator returns a string, which represents the value's type.
The `typeof` operator is not entirely perfect and should only be used when you are sure about how it works. See the following issue:

```
function greetUser( user ) {
 if ( typeof user !== 'object' ) {
   throw new Error('Type is not an object');
 }
 return `Hi, ${user.name}`;
}

console.log('Greet a correct user: ', greetUser( {name: 'Codebeast', age:
24 } ))
// Greet a correct user: Hi, Codebeast

console.log('Greet a boolean: ', greetUser( [1, 2, 3] ))
// Greet a boolean: Hi, undefined
```

You may have expected an error to be thrown when the function was called with an array for the second time. Instead, the program got past the check and executed `user.name` before realizing that it is undefined. Why did it get past this check? Remember that an array is an object. Therefore, we need something more specific to catch the check. Date and regex could have passed the check as well, even though that may not have been the intent.

The toString method

The `toString` method is prototypically inherited by all the objects and wrapped objects (primitives). When you call this method on them, it returns a string token of the type. See the following examples:

```
Object.prototype.toString.call([]); // [object Array]
Object.prototype.toString.call({}); // [object Object]
Object.prototype.toString.call(''); // [object String]
Object.prototype.toString.call(new Date()); // [object Date]
// etc
```

Now you can use this to check the types, as shown by Todd Motto (`https://toddmotto.com/understanding-javascript-types-and-reliable-type-checking/#true-object-types`):

```
var getType = function (elem) {
 return Object.prototype.toString.call(elem).slice(8, -1);
};
var isObject = function (elem) {
 return getType(elem) === 'Object';
```

```
};

// You can use the function
// to check types
if (isObject(person)) {
 person.getName();
}
```

What the preceding example does is check the part of the string returned by the `toString` method to determine its type.

Final Note

The examples we saw previously are just an overkill for a simple type check. If JavaScript had strict type features, we wouldn't have gone through this stress. In fact, this chapter would never have existed.

Imagine that JavaScript could do this:

```
function greet( username: string ) {
 return `Hi, ${username}`;
}
```

We wouldn't have gone through all that type checking hell because the compiler (as well as the editors) would have thrown errors when it encountered type inconsistency.

This is where TypeScript comes in. Luckily, with TypeScript, we can write code that looks like the preceding one, and we can have it transpiled to JavaScript.

Summary

Throughout this book, we will be talking about TypeScript for building not just JavaScript apps but also Angular apps. Angular is a JavaScript framework; therefore, it will be characterized with the discussed limitations unless mitigated with TypeScript.

Now that you know the problem at hand, buckle up while we dig Angular with the possible solutions that TypeScript provides.

So far, so good! We have been able to discuss the following concerns to help us move forward:

- Understanding loose types
- Differences between loose types and strict types
- Challenges of loosely typed programming languages, including JavaScript
- Mitigating the effects of loose types

2
Getting Started with TypeScript

In the previous chapter, we discussed the challenges we may encounter because of the loose-type nature of the JavaScript language. We also saw various attempts of mitigating these challenges, none of which felt natural at all. We also introduced TypeScript as a tool that could help; how TypeScript can help is what we will discuss in this chapter.

The building blocks of TypeScript and its core concepts are matters of the heart, and we need to treat them as such. Therefore, backed with hands-on examples, we will discuss these building blocks, how they work together, and how you can integrate them into your workflow as a JavaScript developer. But first, we need to learn how to set up TypeScript.

In this chapter, we will cover the following topics:

- Creating a TypeScript environment
- Building working examples with TypeScript
- Type Annotation
- ES6 and TypeScript

Setting up TypeScript

The TypeScript setup depends on the context where it will be used. This is because you can integrate it in any JavaScript tools, libraries, and frameworks as long as it's properly configured for the environment. For now, we will focus on the simplest and the most basic setup.

A basic knowledge of Node and its package manager npm is required to get going with TypeScript. It's also required that you install both from the Node website (`https://nodejs.org/en/`).

With Node and npm installed, you can install TypeScript globally using npm via the command line tool:

```
npm install -g typescript
```

If you get a permission warning while trying to install, you can use the `sudo` command:

```
sudo npm install -g typescript
```

You will see the following output if the installation goes well:

To confirm whether the TypeScript installation was successful, you can check the installed version. If a version is shown, then you have a successful installation:

```
tsc -v
```

Therefore, a TypeScript instance on your machine will work as shown ahead:

Hello World

TypeScript files have a `.ts` extension. The extension supports both JavaScript and TypeScript. This means that it is correct to write JavaScript code in a `.ts` file without TypeScript. Let's see an example.

First, make an `index.html` file with the following minimal bootstrap markup:

```html
<!-- Code 2.1.html -->
<html>
 <head>
   <title>Example 2.1: Hello World</title>
   <!-- Include Bootstrap and custom style -->
   <link rel="stylesheet"
href="https://maxcdn.bootstrapcdn.com/bootstrap/3.3.7/css/bootstrap.min.css
">
   <link rel="stylesheet" href="2.1.css">
 </head>
 <body>
   <div class="container">
     <div class="col-md-4 col-md-offset-4 main">
       <h3 class="messenger"></h3>
     </div>
     <div class="col-md-4 col-md-offset-4 main">
       <input type="text" class="form-control">
       <button class="button">Greet</button>
     </div>
   </div>
   <!-- Include JavaScript file -->
   <script src="2.1.js"></script>
 </body>
</html>
```

Notice that the JavaScript file added before the closing tag is *not* a `.ts` file; rather, it's a familiar JavaScript file with a `.js` extension. This doesn't mean that our logic will be written in JavaScript; in fact, it's a TypeScript file named `2.1.ts`:

```typescript
// Code 2.1.ts
(function() {
 var button = document.querySelector('.button');
 var input = document.querySelector('.form-control');
 var messenger = document.querySelector('.messenger');

 button.addEventListener('click', handleButtonClick);

 function handleButtonClick() {
   if(input.value.length === 0) {
```

```
      alert('Please enter your name');
      return;
   }
   // Update messanger
   messenger.innerHTML = 'Hello, ' + input.value;
  }
})();
```

Does anything look weird? No, I don't think so. We're still talking pure JavaScript but just that it lives in a TypeScript file. This shows how TypeScript supports pure JavaScript.

Remember that we are importing `2.1.js` in the `index.html` file and not `2.1.ts`. Therefore, it's time to generate an output that the browser can understand. This is where the TypeScript compiler that we installed via `npm` comes in handy. To compile, enter `cd` into your working directory and run the following command in your command line:

```
tsc 2.1.ts
```

Ignore the warning about the value property. We will fix that soon.

This will generate a compiled `2.1.js` file. As you may have guessed, looking at both shows no syntax difference:

You can then serve your web page with the generated assets using a web server. There are lots of options to help you complete this, but serve is quite popular and stable (https://github.com/zeit/serve). To install serve, run the following command:

```
npm install -g serve
```

Now you can serve directly hosting your index file with the following:

```
serve --port 5000
```

With npm scripts, you can run both the commands concurrently. First, initialize package.json:

```
npm init -y
```

Now, add the following scripts to the JSON:

```
"scripts": {"start": "tsc 2.1.ts -w & serve --port 5000"},
```

We passed in the watched option (-w), so TypeScript can recompile whenever a change is detected in the .ts file.

This is what our example looks like:

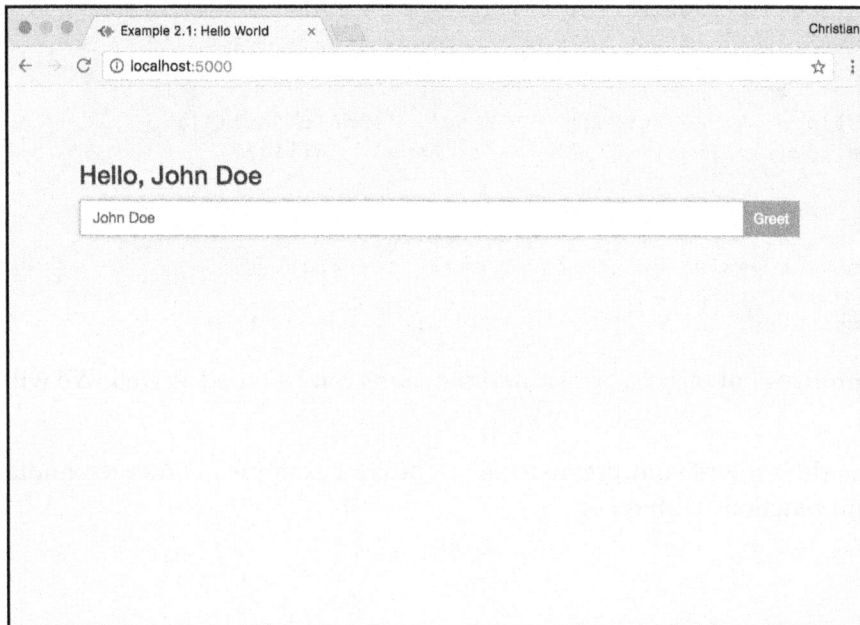

Type annotation in TypeScript

It's worth mentioning again that nothing looks different in the `Hello World` example we just saw. Let's employ some TypeScript specific features, one of which is Types. Types are the reason TypeScript exists, and every other feature apart from Types is just syntactic sugar.

We are not going into details with Types because chapter 3, *Typescript Native Types and Accessors*, covers that. What we can discuss is Type annotation, which is a mechanism that TypeScript uses to apply strict types to a member. Annotation is achieved by following the member initialization with a colon (:) and the type (for example, `string`) as follows:

```
var firstName: string;
```

Let's have a look at some annotated examples:

```
var name: string = 'John';
console.log(name); // John

var age: number = 18;
console.log(age); // 18

var siblings: string[] = ['Lisa', 'Anna', 'Wili'];
console.log(siblings); // ['Lisa', 'Anna', 'Wili']

// OR

var siblings: Array<string> = ['Lisa', 'Anna', 'Wili'];
console.log(siblings); // ['Lisa', 'Anna', 'Wili']

// any type supports all other types
// and useful for objects when we are lazy
// to make types with interfaces/class for them

var attributes: any = {legs: 2, hands: 2, happy: true}
```

Not just primitives but objects, arrays, and functions can be typed as well. We will see how shortly.

What we can do is rewrite our previous `Hello World` example in order to annotate the variables and functions with types.

Take a look at this image again:

On the TypeScript section (right), `value` seems not to be identified by the editor as a property of the DOM and, hence, the error line. But wait, it is the same old JavaScript you have been writing your entire life. What's wrong here?

TypeScript comes with defined types for the DOM. This means that it will throw an error when we try to access a property that is not defined in the respective DOM interface (more on interfaces later). By nature, the DOM query method, `querySelector`, alongside the other query methods return an `Element` type (which is inferred if not annotated). The `Element` type is basic and is comprised of generic information about the DOM, which means that properties and methods specific to what is derived from `Element` will not be seen.

This makes sense not just in TypeScript but also in other OOP languages:

```
class Base {
  name: string = 'John'
}

class Derived extends Base {
  gender: string = 'male'
}
```

```
(new Base()).name // John
(new Base()).gender // throws an error
```

Back to our example, let's see how we can use annotation and casting to fix this:

```
// Code 2.2.ts
(function() {
    // 1. Button type is Element
    var button: Element = document.querySelector('.button');
    // 2. Input type is HTMLInputElement and we cast accordingly
    var input: HTMLInputElement =
<HTMLInputElement>document.querySelector('.form-control');
    // 3. Messanger is HTMLElement and we cast accordingly
    var messenger: HTMLElement = document.querySelector('.messenger') as
HTMLElement;
    // 4. The handler now takes a function and returns another function
(callback)
    button.addEventListener('click', handleButtonClick('Hello,', 'Please
enter your name'));

    function handleButtonClick(prefix, noNameErrMsg) {
        // Logic here
        // Should return a function
    }
})()
```

There are no behavioral changes, just productivity improvements. Let's discuss what's going on:

1. The button element is of type `Element`. Nothing special here because TypeScript already infers that internally.
2. The input element is of the `HTMLInputElement` type. Because TypeScript infers the returned value as `Element`, we had to cast to the correct type, that is, `HTMLInputElement`. This is done by prefixing the returned value with <> and passing the interface that we want to cast it to.
3. The messenger element is of the `HTMLElement` type. We still had to cast here using the same reason as seen in *Step 2* but with a different supported syntax (`as`). `HTMLElement` is a subtype for `Element` and includes more specific DOM properties/methods (such as `innerText`).
4. Rather than passing the callback, we wrap it in a function, so we can receive parameters.

Let's take a look at the method passed to `addEventListener`:

```ts
// Code 2.2.ts
function handleButtonClick(prefix, noNameErrMsg) {
    return function() {
        if(input.value.length === 0) {
            if(typeof noNameErrMsg !== 'string') {
                alert('Something went wrong, and no valid error msg was provided')
                return;
            }
            alert(noNameErrMsg);
            return;
        }

        if(typeof prefix !== 'string') {
            alert('Improper types for prefix or error msg')
        }

        messenger.innerHTML = prefix + input.value;

    }
```

We added a lot of validation logic just to make sure that we are getting the right type from the parameters. We can simplify this by using TypeScript annotation:

```ts
// Code 2.3.ts
function handleButtonClick(prefix: string, noNameErrMsg: string) {
    return function(e: MouseEvent) {
        if(input.value.length === 0) {
            alert(noNameErrMsg);
            return;
        }

        messenger.innerHTML = prefix + input.value;

    }
}
```

This is much better, right? The unnecessary checks are taken care of with Types. In fact, before this gets to the browser, if your editor (for example, VS Code) supports TypeScript, you will get syntax errors when the method is called with invalid types.

Type annotation helps us write less verbose, more comprehensible, and bug-free applications. TypeScript makes annotation flexible; hence, you do not have to strictly provide types for every member in your logic. You're free to annotate what you feel is necessary, ranging from nothing to all; just keep in mind that the more strict your annotations are, the less debugging you will have to do in the browser.

ES6 and beyond

In addition to Type annotation, TypeScript supports EcamaScript 6 (ES6/ES2015) alongside other helpful features, such as enums, decorators, accessibility level (private, public, and protected), interfaces, generics, and so on

We will take a deep look into a few of the features in the next chapter. Before that, let's get our feet wet and our hands a little bit dirty by trying another example, which comprises some of these ES6 and TypeScript-specific features. We will build a counter app. This is just an attempt to get you excited about these features, and you get to see how TypeScript brings the features you always wished existed in JavaScript.

Let's get started with a basic HTML template:

```html
<!-- Code 2.4.html -->
<div class="container">
  <div class="col-md-6 col-md-offset-3 main">
    <div class="row">
      <div class="col-md-4">
        <button id="decBtn">Decrement--</button>
      </div>
      <div class="col-md-4 text-center" id="counter">0</div>
      <div class="col-md-4">
        <button id="incBtn">Inccrement++</button>
      </div>
    </div>
  </div>
</div>
```

User story

The user is expected to increment or decrement a counter from the click of a button, basically, a counter that's initialized to 0, an increment button to increment by 1, and a decrement button to decrement by 1.

Rather than littering our code with DOM manipulations and event logic, we can organize them into classes. After all, that's why classes exist:

```ts
// Code 2.4.ts
class DOM {
  private _incBtn: HTMLElement;
  private _decBtn: HTMLElement;
  private _counter: HTMLElement;

  constructor() {
    this._incBtn = this._getDOMElement('#incBtn');
    this._decBtn = this._getDOMElement('#decBtn');
    this._counter = this._getDOMElement('#counter');
  }


  public _getDOMElement (selector: string) : HTMLElement {
    return document.querySelector(selector) as HTMLElement;
  }

  get incBtn(): HTMLElement {
    return this._incBtn;
  }

  get decBtn(): HTMLElement {
    return this._decBtn;
  }

  get counter(): number {
    return parseInt(this._counter.innerText);
  }

  set counter(value: number) {
    this._counter.innerText = value.toString();
  }
}
```

This is JavaScript looking like a structured language. Let's take some time to explain what is going on:

- First, we create a class and declare some private properties to hold the temporary state of the HTML DOM elements. Visibility features such as `private` are specific to TypeScript only but classes have been around in ES6.
- The constructor uses this `_getDOMElement` private utility method to query the DOM and initialize the values of the private properties.

- The `incBtn` and `decBtn` getters are used to make the values of these private properties public. This is a common pattern in OOP. Getters are categorized under accessors and available in ES6.
- The `counter` accessors are used to set and retrieve the values of the counter text by converting them to integer and string, respectively.

Your first attempt to run this should throw an error, as shown in the following image:

```
GET / 304 1ms
GET /2.4.js 304 1ms
GET /2.4.css 304 1ms
GET / 304 0ms
GET /2.4.js 304 0ms
GET /2.4.css 200 1ms - 445
1:56:49 AM - File change detected. Starting incremental compilation...


2.4.ts(21,9): error TS1056: Accessors are only available when targeting ECMAScript 5 and higher.
2.4.ts(25,9): error TS1056: Accessors are only available when targeting ECMAScript 5 and higher.
2.4.ts(29,9): error TS1056: Accessors are only available when targeting ECMAScript 5 and higher.
2.4.ts(33,9): error TS1056: Accessors are only available when targeting ECMAScript 5 and higher.
1:56:49 AM - Compilation complete. Watching for file changes.
```

This is expected because TypeScript compiles to ES3 by default, but getters and setters (accessors) are not available in ES3. To get rid of this error, you can tell the TypeScript compiler that you prefer ES5 rather than ES3:

```
"start": "tsc 2.4.ts -w -t es5 & serve --port 5000"
```

The `-t` flag, alias for `--target`, tells TypeScript which version to compile to.

The `DOMEvent` class is a lot simpler--just a single method to register all kinds of events when called:

```
// Code 2.4.ts
class DOMEvents {
  private register(htmlElement: HTMLElement, type:string, callback: (e:
Event) => void): void {
    htmlElement.addEventListener(type, callback)
  }
}
```

The method takes the following:

- An element to listen for events on
- The type of event (for example, `click`, `mouseover`, and `dblclick`) as string
- A callback method that returns nothing (`void`) but is passed to the event payload

The method then uses `addEventListener` to register the event.

Finally, we need an entry point for the example. This will be in the form of a class as well and the class will depend on an instance of DOM and DOMEvent classes:

```ts
// Code 2.4.ts
class App {
  constructor(public dom:DOM, public domEvents: DOMEvents) {
    this.setupEvents()
  }
  private setupEvents() {
    const buttons = [this.dom.incBtn, this.dom.decBtn];
    buttons.forEach(button => {
      this.domEvents.register(button, 'click',
this.handleClicks.bind(this))
    })
  }
  private handleClicks(e: MouseEvent): void {
    const {id} = <HTMLElement>e.target;
    if(id === 'incBtn') {
      this.incrementCounter();
    } else {
      this.decrementCounter();
    }
  }

  private incrementCounter() {
    this.dom.counter++
  }

  private decrementCounter () {
    this.dom.counter--
  }
}
```

Let's discuss how the preceding snippet works:

- The constructor, which is called when the class is initialized, attempts to set up events using the `setupEvents` method.
- The `setupEvents` method iterates over the list of buttons that we have on the DOM and calls the `DOMEvents register` method on each of them

- The register method is passed to the button as `HTMLElement`, `click` as the type of event, and `handleClicks` as the event handler. The handler is bound with the right contextual `this`. This is always a confusion in JavaScript; Yehuda Katz has explained how it works in a simple manner at `http://yehudakatz.com/2011/08/11/understanding-javascript-function-invocation-and-this/`.
- The callback method invokes `incrementCounter` or `decrementCounter` depending on the ID of the button that is clicked. These methods add or subtract `1` from the counter, respectively.

You can initialize the app by creating an instance of `App`:

```
// Code 2.4.ts
(new App(new DOM, new DOMEvents))
```

The image shows our newly built slick counter app:

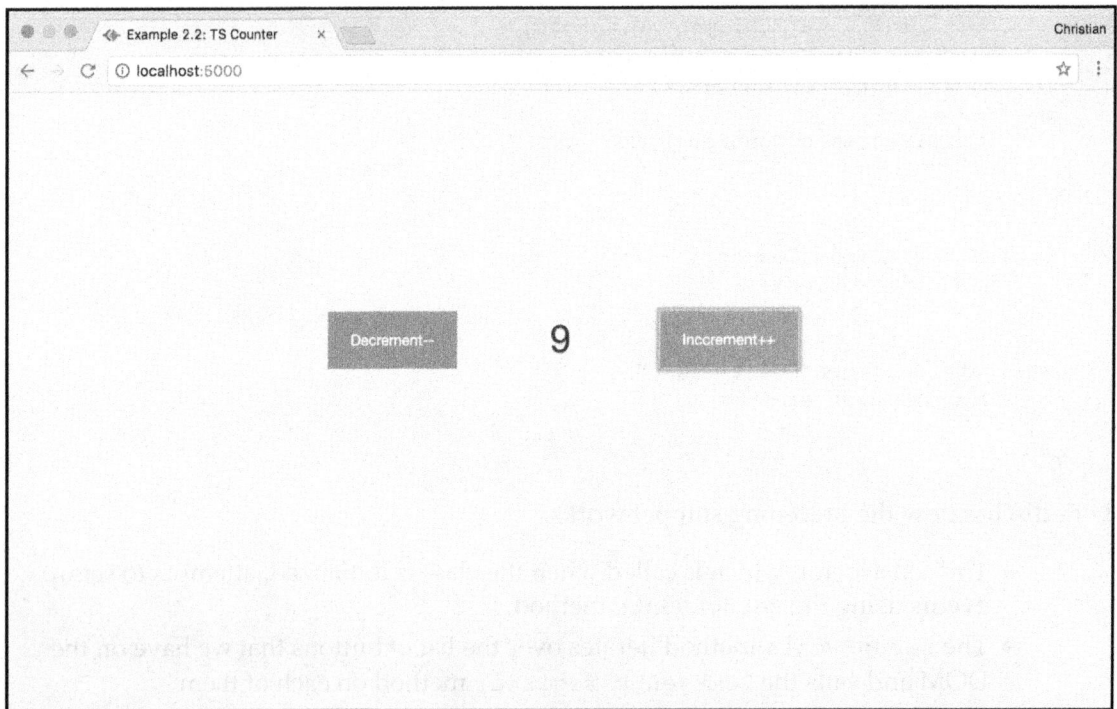

Final notes

It's important to point out the cool features we used in these examples once more:

- Classes
- Accessors
- Visibility
- Arrow functions (callbacks):

```
var fooFunc = (arg1) => {
    return arg1
}
```

- The `const` keyword for variable declarations instead of `var`
- Destructuring :

```
const {id} = <HTMLElement>e.target;
```

Summary

Some of these features are available natively in the JavaScript environment; TypeScript builds on them to give you a better experience as a developer. This is why it is called a JavaScript superset.

In the next chapter, we will sit back to review and describe these features with more examples to make you get used to the workflow.

3

Typescript Native Types and Features

You have seen different kinds of examples of using TypeScript. Hopefully, you now know what TypeScript can offer you as a developer. There are still some TypeScript core concepts to learn before hopping right into using it to build Angular 2 apps. This chapter will cover the following TypeScript concepts:

- Basic types, such as strings, numbers, Boolean, arrays, void, and so on
- Function types
- Interfaces
- Decorators

Basic types

Let's revisit the basic types. Most of the types that we will be discussing are familiar to you from JavaScript, but it's nice to have a refresher session to better appreciate what TypeScript offers. Some of the types, on the other hand, are not available in JavaScript but are TypeScript-specific.

Strings

Strings are available in both JavaScript and TypeScript. They are used to represent textual data. This data appears in programs as string literals. These literals are easily identified in most programming languages because of the wrapping double quotes (""). In JavaScript (and TypeScript), the literals are represented with both double quotes ("") and single quotes (''):

```
let text: string = "Hi, I am a string. Now you know!";
```

In the preceding snippet, the text variable stores this string: "Hi, I am a string. Now you know!". Because TypeScript supports the latest features of JavaScript, you can use the new ES6 template literal:

```
const outro: string = 'Now you know!';

let text: string = `Hi, I am not just a simple string.
                    I am actually a paragraph. ${outro}`;
```

Numbers

Numbers are available in JavaScript and TypeScript. Numbers represent floating numbers in JavaScript. You feed them right in with the keyboard, without any decoration like we had to do for strings:

```
let whole: number = 6;
let decimal: number = 2.5;
let hex: number = 0xf00d;
let binary: number = 0b1010;
let octal: number = 0o744;
```

Boolean

The Boolean type is available in JavaScript and TypeScript. Booleans are the simplest types you will ever meet in a programming language. They answer the question with yes or no, which is represented in JavaScript as true or false:

```
let isHappy: boolean = true;
let done: boolean = false;
```

Arrays

Arrays are available in both JavaScript and TypeScript. Data structures in JavaScript are basically represented with objects and arrays. Objects are key-value pairs while arrays have an indexable structure. There is no `array` type, rather you provide types for the items that are contained in an array.

You have two options for doing this. You can use the `[]` symbol pair, as follows:

```
let textArray: string[];

textArray = ["java", "kotlin", "typescript", "the rest..."]
```

Alternatively, you can use the built-in generic type:

```
let numberArray: Array<number> = [9, 8, 7, 6, 5, 4, 3, 2, 1, 0]
```

Void

Void is available *only* in TypeScript. The `void` type is applicable to functions' return types (we will discuss this soon). Void indicates that a function is not expected to return anything:

```
let sum: number = 20

// No return type function
function addToGlobalSum(numToAdd): void {
    number + numToAdd
}

addToGlobalSum(30)
console.log(number) // 50
```

Any

Any is available *only* in TypeScript. The `any` type is the most flexible type. It allows you to get closer to the loose nature of JavaScript when there is a need for it. Such needs could arise from third-party libraries that are not typed and if you don't know which value type may be returned from a property or method.

This type can store all the known JavaScript types:

```
// Stores a string
let name: any = 'John Doe'

// Stores a number
let age: any = 24

// Stores a boolean
let employed: any = true

// ...even data structures
let person: any[] =['John Doe', 24, true]
```

Tuple

Tuples are available *only* in TypeScript. They allow you to have varying types in an array. Tuples come with the implication that the fixed number of elements in an array must be defined while creating the type. For example, if we need an array of string, number, and boolean, it will look like this:

```
let flexibleArray: [string, number, boolean];

flexibleArray = ['John Doe', 24, true]
```

When you try to access an index that was not initially created, the new index is added with the appropriate inferred type:

```
let anotherFlexArray: [string, number];

anotherFlexArray = ['John Doe', 24];

Assign true to index 2
anotherFlexArray[2] = true;

// anotherFlexArray becomes ['John Doe', 24, true]
```

Enums

Enums are available *only* in TypeScript. On a few occasions, you may simply want to store a set of numbers, serially or not. Enums hand you a numeric data structure control without having to drag in the complexities of arrays or objects.

The following example shows an enum type with numbers from 0 to 2:

```
enum Status {Started, InProgress, Completed}

let status:Status = Status.InProgress // 1
```

Enums are 0-based; therefore, Started holds 0, InProgress holds 1, and Completed holds 2. In addition, enums are flexible; hence, you can provide a number for the starting point instead of 0:

```
enum Status {Started = 1, InProgress, Completed}

let status:Status = Status.InProgress // 2
```

You can write more expressive code with Enums. Let's see how, by using percentage values for the status in the preceding example:

```
enum Status {Started = 33, InProgress = 66, Completed = 100}

let status:Status = Status.InProgress + '% done' // 66% done
```

It's easy to find out the name of the value if you know the actual value:

```
enum Status {Started = 33, InProgress = 66, Completed = 100}

let status:string = Status[66] // InProgress
```

Functions and function types

JavaScript functions are loosely typed and are some of the most common sources of errors in the language. This is what a basic function looks like:

```
function stringToArray(char) {
  return char.split(' ')
}
```

How sure are we that `char` is not a number? Well, we might not have any control over what the developer consuming `stringToArray` will pass in. This is why we need to be strict about the value types using TypeScript.

Functions use types in two different parts of their declaration:

1. Function parameters
2. Function return value

Function parameters

You can tell TypeScript what type of values a function should expect, and it will strictly adhere to it. The following example shows a function that receives a typed string and a number as its parameters:

```
// Typed parameters
function stringIndex(char: string, index: number) {
  const arr = char.split(' ')
  return arr[number];
}
```

The `char` and `index` parameters have the `string` and `number` types, respectively. Even before things get to the browser, TypeScript will alert you when you try something silly:

```
function stringIndex(char: string, index: number) {
 const arr = char.split(' ')
 return arr[number];
 }

stringIndex(true, 'silly') // Types don't match
```

Of course, function expressions are not left out:

```
const stringIndex = function (char: string, index: number) {
 const arr = char.split(' ')
 return arr[number];
 }
```

Moreover, arrow functions are welcome too:

```
const stringIndex = (char: string, index: number) => char.split('
')[number];
```

Function return value

The value expected from a function when it is executed can also be strictly typed:

```
function stringIndex(char: string, index: number): string {
 const arr = char.split(' ')
 return arr[number];
}
```

As you can see from the preceding code snippet, the return type comes after the brackets containing the parameters and before the opening curly bracket of the function's body. The preceding function is expected to, and must, return a string. Anything other than a string will scream at you with errors.

Optional parameters

When a function's parameter is strictly typed, it feels rigid when the function needs to be flexible. Why should we pass in `index` to our previous example in a situation where we intend to return the whole string if the index is missing?

When the index parameter is omitted while calling the function, TypeScript will throw an error. To overcome this issue, we can declare the `index` parameter as optional:

```
function stringIndex(char: string, index?: number): string {
   // Just return string as is
   // if index is not passed in
   if(!index) return char;
   // else, return the index
   // that was passed in
   const arr = char.split(' ')
   return arr[number];
}
```

The question mark succeeding the parameter name tells TypeScript that it's okay if the parameter is missing when called. Be careful to handle such cases of parameters not being supplied in the function body, as shown in the preceding example.

Interfaces

Interfaces are contracts that our code adheres too. It's an agreement that data structures must follow. This helps every data/logic implementing an interface stay safe from improper or non-matching types. It also validates the types and availability of values passed in.

In TypeScript, interfaces are used for the following:

1. Creating types for JavaScript objects.
2. Setting up contracts for classes to adhere to.

We will discuss how interfaces are applied in the scenarios we just listed.

Interfaces for JavaScript object types

We agree that the following is a valid JavaScript object:

```
// Option bag
let options = {show: true, container: '#main'};
```

It is a valid JavaScript code but loosely typed. All this while, we have been discussing strings, numbers, Boolean, and even arrays. We are yet to consider objects.

As you may have imagined, the following code snippet demonstrates a typed version of the preceding example:

```
// Typed object
let options: {show: boolean, container: string};

// Assing values
options = {show: true, container: '#main'};
```

This is correct in fact, but TypeScript could use interfaces to make it more maintainable and easy to comprehend. The following is how we write interfaces in TypeScript:

```
interface OptionBag {
  show: boolean,
  container: string
}
```

What you can then do is make the `options` variable of the `OptionBag` type:

```
// Typed object
let options: OptionBag = {show: true, container: '#main'};
```

Optional properties

One thing about interfaces, though, is that the defined properties/methods of an interface must be supplied when creating the values that are typed with that interface. Basically, I am saying that we must adhere strictly to the contract established with an interface.

Therefore, the following is incorrect and will throw an error:

```
interface OptionBag {
 show: boolean,
 container: string
}


let options: OptionBag = {show: true}; // Error
```

We can make `container` optional; we use the question mark literal, as seen in a previous example:

```
interface OptionBag {
 show: boolean,
 container?: string
}


let options: OptionBag = {show: true}; // No Error
```

Be careful, though, to account for when the optional parameter is not supplied. The following is an example that does so:

```
// Get element
function getContainerElement(options: OptionBag):HTMLElement {
   let containerElement: HTMLElement
   if(!options.container) {
      // container was not passed in
      containerElement = document.querySelector('body');
   } else {
      // container was passed in
      containerElement = document.querySelector(options.container);
   }

   return containerElement
}
```

Read-only properties

Another typical situation is when you have properties to which you intend to assign values only once, just like we do with the ES6 `const` declaration keyword. You can mark the values as `readonly`:

```
interface StaticSettings {
   readonly width: number,
   readonly height: number
}
```

```
// There are no problems here
let settings: StaticSettings = {width: 1500, height: 750}

// ...but this will throw an error
settings.width = 1000
// or
settings.height = 500
```

Interfaces as contracts

You can ensure that a class adheres to a particular contract using interfaces. I use the term contract in the sense that all the properties and methods defined in the interface must be implemented in the class.

Let's assume that we have the following Note interface:

```
interface Note {
  wordCount: number
}
```

To implement the interface using a class, we add the implements keyword after the class name followed by the interface we are implementing:

```
class NoteTaker implements Note {
  // Implement wordCount from
  // Note interface
  wordCount: number;
  constructor(count: number) {
    this.wordCount = count
  }
}
```

Interfaces do not only define the signatures for properties but they also accept function types as methods:

```
interface Note {
  wordCount: number;
  updateCount(count: number): void
}
```

This could be implemented by a class in the following way:

```
class NoteTaker implements Note {
 // Implement wordCount from
 // Note interface
 wordCount: number;
```

```
  constructor(count: number) {
    this.wordCount = count
  }

  updateCount(count: number): void {
    wordCount += count
  }
}
```

TypeScript will throw an error if neither the `wordCount` property nor the `updateCount` method exists in the `NoteTaker` class.

Decorators

The most common feature introduced in Angular 2+ is **decorators**. Decorators, at first glance, are confusing because of the unusual @ sign preceding their usage:

```
app.component.ts — Just-comments

TS  app.component.ts ✕

 1    import {Component, OnInit} from '@angular/core';
 2    import {CommentService} from "./comment.service";
 3    import {Observable} from "rxjs";
 4    import {DsService} from "./ds.service";
 5
 6    @Component({
 7      selector: 'app-root',
 8      templateUrl: './app.component.html',
 9      styleUrls: ['./app.component.css']
10    })
11    export class AppComponent implements OnInit{
12
13      public title = 'Just Comments!';
14      public comments: Array<any>;
15
16      constructor(
17        private commentService: CommentService,
18        private dsService: DsService
```

master ⚙ ⊗ 0 ⚠ 0 ⓘ 1   Ln 1, Col 1   Spaces: 2   UTF-8   LF   TypeScript   2.3.4

The preceding screenshot is a code snippet from an Angular application. It shows a component decorator decorating a class called `AppComponent`.

At first, this might look overwhelming because, in the history of JavaScript, I have never seen the @ literal used this way. If only we knew it was just a function that had access to the members of what it is decorating! Classes, properties, methods, and accessors are all allowed to be decorated. Let's discuss how to decorate methods and classes

Decorating methods

Let's assume that we want to make a method on a class read-only. Therefore, after creating the method, it cannot be overridden for any reason. For example, this is what the method looks like:

```
class Report {
  errPayload;

 // To become readonly
  error() {
     console.log(`The following error occured ${errPayload}`)
  }
}
```

If we do not want to override `error` in the application's lifecycle, we could write a decorator to set the descriptor's `writable` property to `false`:

```
function readonly(target, key, descriptor) {
   descriptor.writable = false;
   return descriptor
}
```

The common signature is that a method decorator takes the same parameters as `Object.defineProperty`. In such a case, the target will be the class, the key will be the method name, which is a property of the class, and the descriptor will be the `config` object.

We can now decorate the `error` method with the just created `readonly` decorator:

```
class Report {
 errPayload;

 // Decorated method
 @readonly
 error() {
    console.log(`The following error occured ${errPayload}`)
 }
}
```

Any attempt to mutate the error property will fail:

```
const report = new Report()

// This would never work
// because 'error' is read only
report.error = function() {
   console.log('I won't even be called')
}
```

Decorating classes

Another commonly decorated member is the class. In fact, in Angular, almost all classes (components, services, modules, filters, and directives) are decorated. This is why it is important to understand the importance of the existence of decorators.

Decorators can be used to extend the features of a class, as shown in the following example:

```
// decorator function
function config(target) {
  target.options = {
    id: '#main',
    show: true
  }
}

// class
@config
class App {}

// options added
console.log(App.options) // {id: '#main', show: true}
```

Decorator factories

The preceding example is rigid because the `options` object will always have the same value. What if we needed to receive dynamic values? Of course, that's a valid question to ask because the `id` property may not always be `#main`. Therefore, we need to be more flexible.

Decorator factories are functions that return a decorator, giving you the power to pass in arguments for the decorator via its factory:

```
// decorator factory function
function config(options) {
  // decorator function
  return function(target) {
    target.options = options
  }
}

// class decorator
// with arguments
@config({id: '#main', show: true})
class App {}

// options added
console.log(App.options) // {id: '#main', show: true}
```

Summary

We spent time in the first three chapters discussing TypeScript fundamentals with the intention that while walking through the rest of the chapters (which are filled with a lot of Angular stuff), TypeScript will be something you don't have to worry about.

It is fine to assume that the basic types, function types, decorators, and interfaces have been added to your existing knowledge of TypeScript.

In the coming chapters of this book, we will soak ourselves in Angular. If you have come this far, then you made it through the boring parts of this book because, henceforth, we will be building a lot of fun examples with Angular 2+.

4
Up and Running with Angular and TypeScript

The previous chapters set out to explain the basic and most common features of TypeScript. These features will be used extensively while working on Angular projects. TypeScript is completely optional when it comes to building Angular projects but, trust me, just using JavaScript is not a route you will want to take after experiencing how TypeScript simplifies the development story.

This chapter introduces us to the exciting part of this book--building Angular apps with TypeScript. We will cover the following topics in this chapter:

- Setting up Angular with TypeScript
- Understanding component basics
- Learning about Angular's template syntax
- Some data binding magic

All these exciting topics will be backed with good examples, so you can see for yourself how these things work. Let's get started.

Setting up Angular and TypeScript

Angular is not such a difficult framework to get started with. Unfortunately, from a beginner's perspective, the ecosystem may overwhelm you with lots and lots of terms. Most of these terms represent the tools that make Angular work, and not Angular itself. Webpack, linters, TypeScript, typings, build processes, and so on, are some confusing terms that may turn you off at the beginning of your Angular journey.

For this reason, the Angular team built an all-in-one tool to help you pay less attention to those surrounding tools but more attention to building your project. It's known as the Angular CLI, and with just a few CLI commands you're building your app. The time spent on managing JavaScript tools these days is alarming, and you don't want to get caught up in that mess as a beginner (or even a professional).

To install the CLI, you need to run the following command with npm:

```
npm install -g @angular/cli
```

When the installation is complete, you should see the following npm log in the console:

You can check whether the installation was successful by running the `help` or `version` commands:

```
# Help command
ng help

# Version command
ng version
```

The help command will show a list of commands available via the CLI tool, while the version command will show the currently installed version. None of them will print the aforementioned information if the installation was unsuccessful.

Here are the printed log details when you run the `help` command:

Running the version command shows the following screenshot:

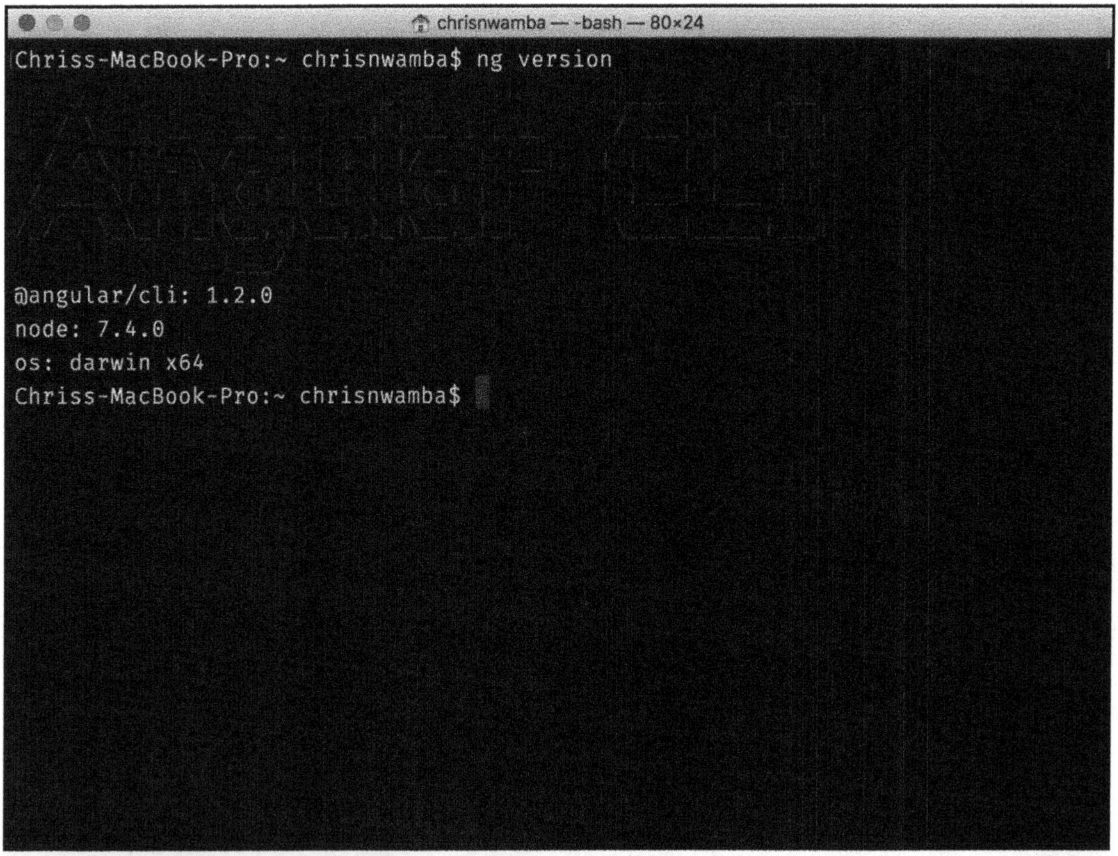

```
Chriss-MacBook-Pro:~ chrisnwamba$ ng version




@angular/cli: 1.2.0
node: 7.4.0
os: darwin x64
Chriss-MacBook-Pro:~ chrisnwamba$
```

Creating a new Angular project

With the CLI installed, you can now start using it on your project. The first thing, of course, is to create one. The CLI's new command is used just once in a project to generate the starter files and configuration that the project needs:

```
ng new hello-angular
```

The command does not just create a project for you; it also installs the npm dependencies, so you do not have to run the install command before getting started:

```
create src/index.html
create src/main.ts
create src/polyfills.ts
create src/styles.css
create src/test.ts
create src/tsconfig.app.json
create src/tsconfig.spec.json
create src/typings.d.ts
create .angular-cli.json
create e2e/app.e2e-spec.ts
create e2e/app.po.ts
create e2e/tsconfig.e2e.json
create .gitignore
create karma.conf.js
create package.json
create protractor.conf.js
create tsconfig.json
create tslint.json
Installing packages for tooling via npm.
Installed packages for tooling via npm.
Directory is already under version control. Skipping initialization of git.
You can `ng set --global packageManager=yarn`.
Project 'hello-angular' successfully created.
Chriss-MacBook-Pro:Chapter4 chrisnwamba$
```

Navigate right to the root of the folder and run the `serve` command:

```
ng serve
```

You will get the following output after running the command, which shows that your app is running successfully and where you can access it. It also shows bundled files, including styles and scripts. Note that there are no TypeScript files here; everything has been converted to JavaScript for the browser to understand:

```
** NG Live Development Server is listening on localhost:4200, open your browser on http://localhost:
4200 **
Hash: 9cd10bb4017fe1eabf60
Time: 6606ms
chunk    {0} polyfills.bundle.js, polyfills.bundle.js.map (polyfills) 160 kB {4} [initial] [rendered
]
chunk    {1} main.bundle.js, main.bundle.js.map (main) 5.28 kB {3} [initial] [rendered]
chunk    {2} styles.bundle.js, styles.bundle.js.map (styles) 10.5 kB {4} [initial] [rendered]
chunk    {3} vendor.bundle.js, vendor.bundle.js.map (vendor) 2.18 MB [initial] [rendered]
chunk    {4} inline.bundle.js, inline.bundle.js.map (inline) 0 bytes [entry] [rendered]
webpack: Compiled successfully.
```

You should see your shiny app running at `localhost:4200`:

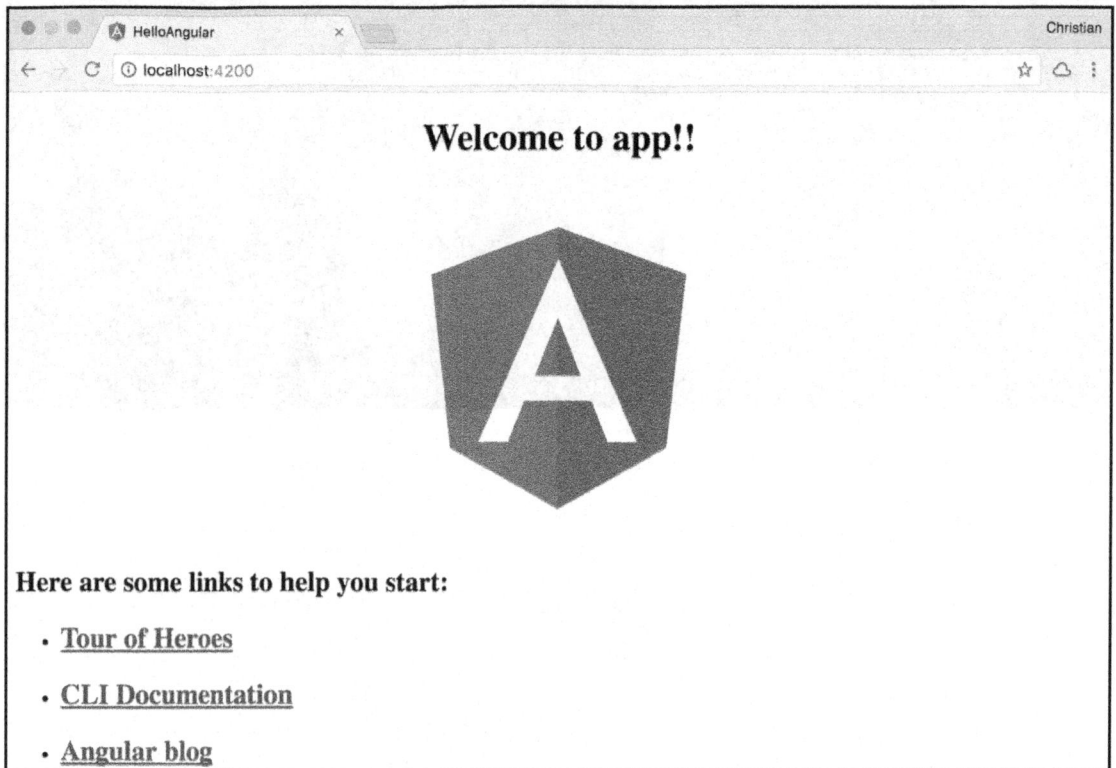

Project structure

Angular generates a lot of helper files to facilitate testing, the build process, package management, and so on. You can build a successful project without ever caring about what these files do. Hence, we are just going to show a few of the files that are important for us to get started:

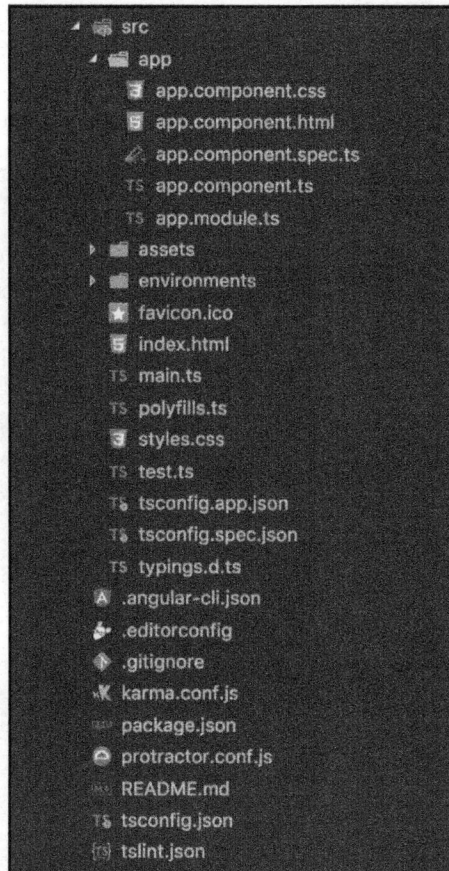

```
▲ 🗔 src
  ▲ 📁 app
        🎨 app.component.css
        🔲 app.component.html
        ✏️ app.component.spec.ts
        TS app.component.ts
        TS app.module.ts
  ▶ 📁 assets
  ▶ 📁 environments
      ⭐ favicon.ico
      🔲 index.html
      TS main.ts
      TS polyfills.ts
      🎨 styles.css
      TS test.ts
      TS tsconfig.app.json
      TS tsconfig.spec.json
      TS typings.d.ts
      Ⓐ .angular-cli.json
      ✒️ .editorconfig
      🔺 .gitignore
      ⚛️ karma.conf.js
      📦 package.json
      ⚙️ protractor.conf.js
      README.md
      TS tsconfig.json
      {ts} tslint.json
```

We should be concerned about the `src` directory for now. That's where our project files (components, services, templates, and so on) will live.

Generating files

You can add more TypeScript files and templates manually, but it is more effective to do so with the CLI tool. This is because the CLI tool not only creates files but also generates starter snippets to represent the kind of file you are trying to create. For example, let's create a quote component:

```
ng generate component quote
# OR
ng g component quote
```

This is what the component command looks like with some of the generated codes and files:

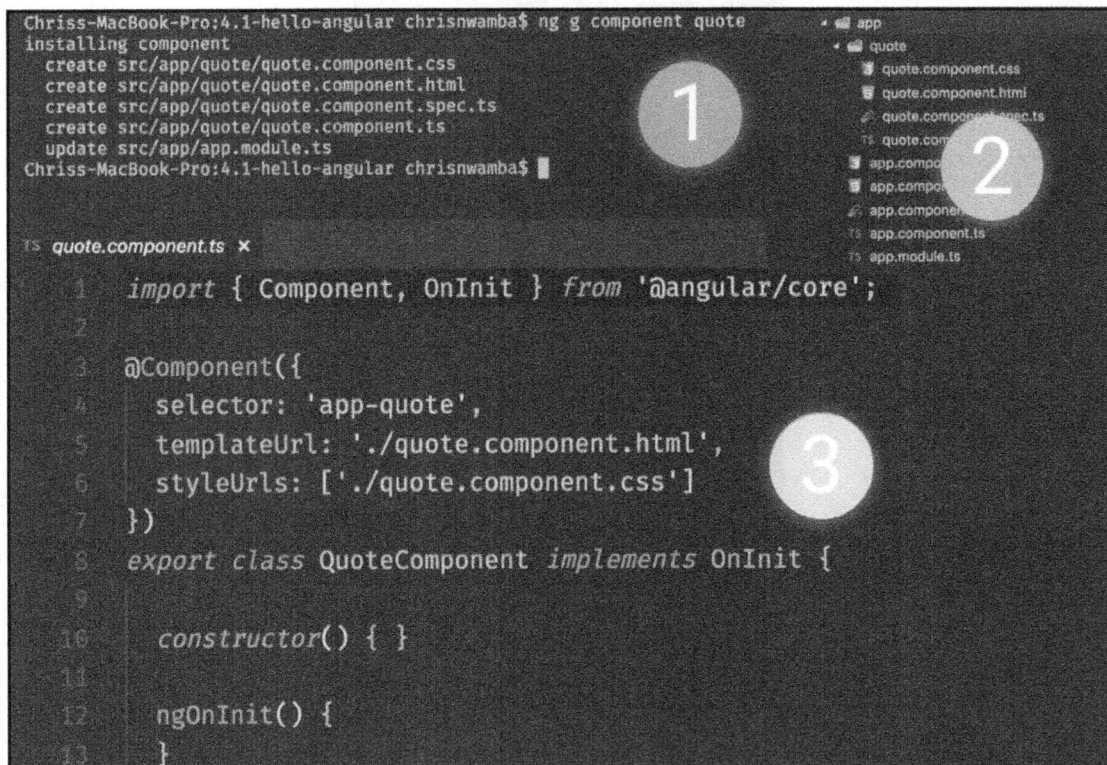

The image comprises of the following:

1. The CLI output of the generation process.
2. The generated component, template, CSS, and test files.
3. The TypeScript component.

The CLI can be used to generate other Angular/TypeScript building blocks, not just components. We won't try it out right now; we will do so while discussing it in topics in upcoming chapters. The following table is to generate commands as seen on the project's Github readme:

Scaffold	Usage
Component	`ng g component my-new-component`
Directive	`ng g directive my-new-directive`
Pipe	`ng g pipe my-new-pipe`
Service	`ng g service my-new-service`
Class	`ng g class my-new-class`
Guard	`ng g guard my-new-guard`
Interface	`ng g interface my-new-interface`
Enum	`ng g enum my-new-enum`
Module	`ng g module my-module`

Basics concepts

We will delve into different topics in this book, but it is a good idea to roughly explain what is going on for the sake of context.

Components

Your curiosity may have led you into opening `app.component.ts` or `quote.component.ts`. Don't worry if they seemed overwhelming; we will discuss components extensively in this book (especially, in the next two chapters).

Components are the heart of any Angular project. They are the core building blocks, and every other feature is just meant to support components. The files mentioned contain Angular components written in TypeScript. This is what `app.component.ts` looks like:

```
import { Component } from '@angular/core';

@Component({
  selector: 'app-root',
  templateUrl: './app.component.html',
  styleUrls: ['./app.component.css']
})
export class AppComponent {  title = 'app'; }
```

A component is a decorated class with a template. The type of decoration is what matters, in this case, a `Component` decorator. Remember from the previous chapter that decorators are just functions that extend the feature they are decorating. That is what is happening in the preceding example.

First, we import this decorator from Angular's core module, `@angular/core`. We then place the decorator right above our `AppComponent` class. The decorator takes a JavaScript object as its argument to describe the component. The object contains the following:

- `selector`: This is what the component will be identified as when it is called in any part of the app. Because this component is the entry point of your app, it will be used directly in the body by including its selector:

  ```
  <!--./src/index.html-->
  ...
  <body>
    <app-root></app-root>
  </body>
  ...
  ```

- `templateUrl`: Components render a template to the view. We need a way to tell the component which template to render. This is possible via the `template` or `templateUrl` property. The `template` property takes a string of HTML content while `templateUrl` takes a URL to the template HTML file.
- `styleUrls`: This is an array of style Urls that are applied to the defined template.

The class that is the actual component (and is being decorated) becomes the home for properties and methods that are associated with this component. All these work together as one, to make a reusable feature called a component.

The quote component looks very much alike:

```
import { Component, OnInit } from '@angular/core';

@Component({
  selector: 'app-quote',
  templateUrl: './quote.component.html',
  styleUrls: ['./quote.component.css']
})
export class QuoteComponent implements OnInit {
  constructor() { }
  ngOnInit() {  }
}
```

The only obvious difference is that it implements the `OnInit` interface, which has an `ngOnInit` method that the class must implement. This method is known as a lifecycle hook, which we will discuss soon.

Templates

Templates are just regular HTML files, though supercharged with interpolation and directives. The following is the current content of `app.component.html`, which is the template for `AppComponent`:

```
<div style="text-align:center">
  <h1>  Welcome to {{title}}!!  </h1>
  <img width="300" src="...">
</div>
<h2>Here are some links to help you start: </h2>
<ul>
  <li>  <h2><a target="_blank" href="https://angular.io/tutorial">Tour of
Heroes</a></h2>  </li>
  <li>  <h2><a target="_blank"
href="https://github.com/angular/angular-cli/wiki">CLI
Documentation</a></h2>  </li>
  <li>  <h2><a target="_blank" href="http://angularjs.blogspot.ca/">Angular
blog</a></h2>  </li>
</ul>
```

As you can see, it's just the usual HTML. One thing might seem unfamiliar, though:

```
<h1>  Welcome to {{title}}!!  </h1>
```

The `title` text wrapped with double curly braces may confuse you. This is called interpolation. The `title` value is resolved at runtime based on the value of a property on the component's class. Don't forget we have a title property with the value, `app`:

```
title = 'app';
```

Apart from binding values like this, you can perform a lot of amazing tasks on the template. They include the following:

- Property and event binding
- Two-way binding
- Iteration and conditions
- Style and class binding
- Simple expressions
- Pipes and directives

Rather than feeding you with all the boring stuff related to templates and template syntax, what we should do is discuss them and how they are related to other upcoming topics. This way, you can see them live in examples, which should be more fun.

Component styles

Components parade reusability a lot. In fact, that's the first answer you get when you ask about the benefits of using the component architecture. This is the reason why templates and styles are scoped to the component rather than littering the app's environment with heavy HTML and CSS.

The `styleUrls` property in the component's decorator argument takes an array of URLs pointing to the styles you want to apply to the component. Most of the time, you just need a single file; therefore, the array will only contain a single URL item, in our case, `app.component.css`. It's currently empty but we can carry out an experiment with it:

```
* {
  background: red;
}
```

The * selector is supposed to select everything in the document. So, we say, *select every element and set the background to red*. You may actually be surprised at the result:

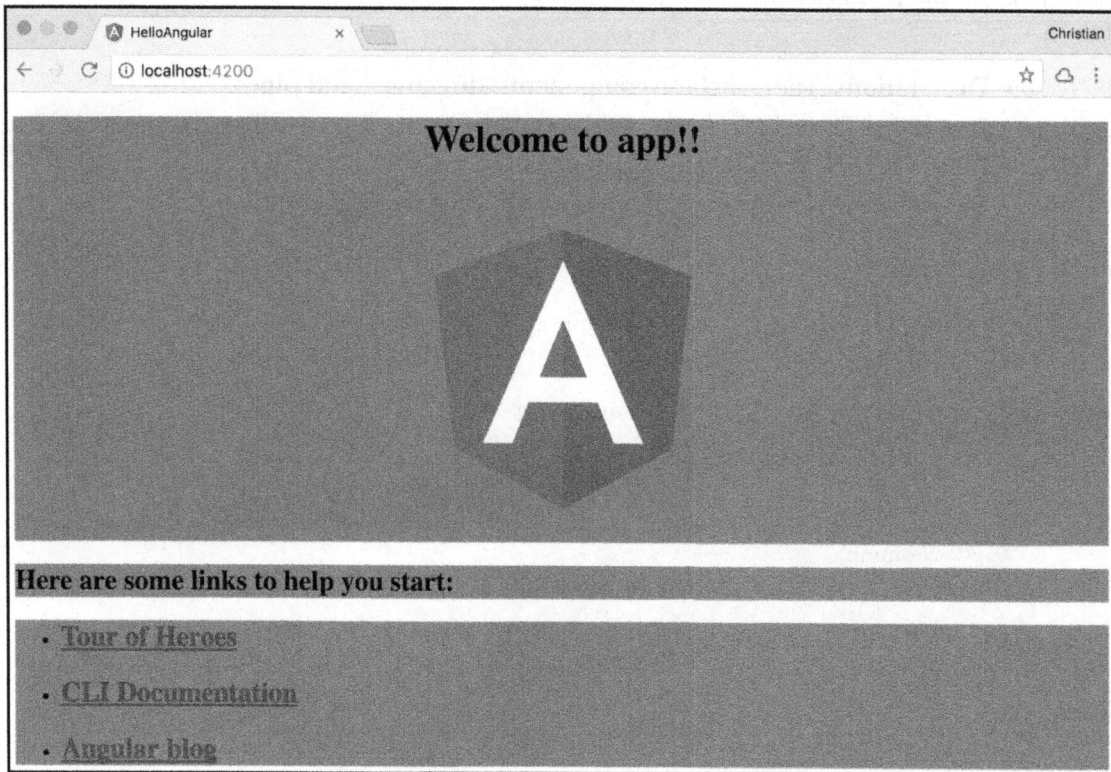

Notice how the actual body tag is not styled, which may not make any outright sense because you used the global selector. Component styles are scoped to the component; therefore the styles cannot leak to the containing parent. This is why the body remains white and the contents in the AppComponent template are red.

Modules

Components are for building small reusable features in your product. They work together with concepts such as services, directives, pipes, and so on, to make a functional feature. In some situations, you may want these features to be moved around from one project to another or even between different sections of a huge project. Therefore, you need a way to collect them together as a feature. This is exactly what modules do.

Modules are classes decorated with the `NgModule` decorator. The decorator takes an object, just like the component decorator. This object describes all the feature members that you need to associate to this module. The possible members (but not all members) are as follows:

- **Declarations**: These include components, directives, and pipes
- **Providers**: These include injectable services
- **Imports**: These include other imported modules
- **Bootstrap**: This is the entry component to start the app with

We have one module already, which is `AppModule`:

```
import { BrowserModule } from '@angular/platform-browser';
import { NgModule } from '@angular/core';

import { AppComponent } from './app.component';
import { QuoteComponent } from './quote/quote.component';

@NgModule({
  declarations: [
    AppComponent,
    QuoteComponent
  ],
  imports: [
    BrowserModule
  ],
  providers: [],
  bootstrap: [
    AppComponent
  ]
})
export class AppModule { }
```

Let's take some time to describe the items in this module:

- **Declarations**: `AppComponent` and `QuoteComponent` are components. Therefore, they fall into this category. One amazing thing that the Angular CLI did after generating the quote component was to add it to the declarations automatically for us. If not, even when you use the component selector somewhere in the app, the quote component contents will still not be displayed, and you will get an error in the console.
- **Imports**: `BrowserModule` is a module. It is a module that contains common browser tasks, especially directives for templates, such as `*ngFor` and more.

- **Providers**: Since we don't have any services yet, the providers can be omitted or the array can be left empty.
- **Bootstrap**: The app module is our entry module. Therefore, it should define the entry component, which is AppComponent. This is what the bootstrap property does.

Unit testing

Although we won't cover testing until the last chapter of this book, it pays to make testing a habit. This is why we are going to explore the simplicity of testing components here.

Basically, Angular provides an abstraction layer for testing your components with the help of TestBed. You don't need to run your entire application before you can see whether your components behave as planned. A simple test comes bundled with the CLI scaffold for our app component. It can be found adjacent to the file (which is a common and good practice) as app.component.spec.ts.

Let's view the contents of this file:

```
import { TestBed, async } from '@angular/core/testing';
import { AppComponent } from './app.component';

describe('AppComponent', () => {

});
```

First, we import the testing utilities from @angular/core/testing and the component to be tested, that is, AppComponent. A describe block, which houses the sets of test suites for a given feature (AppComponent), is also created but left empty.

Before we start writing the suites, we need to configure a temporary testing module for the component. This is done in a beforeEach block:

```
//...
describe('AppComponent', () => {
  beforeEach(async(() => {
    TestBed.configureTestingModule({
      declarations: [ AppComponent ],
    }).compileComponents();
  }));
  // ...
});
```

In the actual app, we could afford the luxury of creating AppModule where AppComponent lives as a declaration. Here, we just need a simple module with AppComponent on it, thanks to the configureTestingModule module of TestBed making this possible.

Next, we can start writing the test suites for whatever scenario we want to examine. First, let's check whether AppComponent is a thing:

```
describe('AppComponent', () => {
  it('should create the app', async(() => {
    const fixture = TestBed.createComponent(AppComponent);
    const app = fixture.debugElement.componentInstance;
    expect(app).toBeTruthy();
  }));
});
```

We first try to create an instance of the component with componentInstance after creating the component itself with createComponent().

The actual check is done when we assert with expect to see whether the component exists with toBeTruthy().

We can also check the content of the component's properties:

```
it(`should have as title 'app'`, async(() => {
  const fixture = TestBed.createComponent(AppComponent);
  const app = fixture.debugElement.componentInstance;
  expect(app.title).toEqual('app');
}));
```

With app being an instance of the component, you can access the properties and methods on this instance. We just tested to see whether the initial value of app.title is equal to app.

The last test suite actually checks the DOM for values:

```
it('should render title in a h1 tag', async(() => {
  const fixture = TestBed.createComponent(AppComponent);
  fixture.detectChanges();
  const compiled = fixture.debugElement.nativeElement;
  expect(compiled.querySelector('h1').textContent).toContain('Welcome to
app!!');  }));
```

Note that `detectChanges` is called in this suite. This kicks off binding, if any, on the template. Then, instead of creating an instance, we grab hold of the compiled element, query it for the `h1` tag, and check whether the text content of the tag contains `Welcome to app`.

To run these tests, execute the following command:

```
ng test
```

This should start Karma, an isolated test environment. Your tests will run and the following will be printed to the CLI:

```
Chriss-MacBook-Pro:4.1-hello-angular chrisnwamba$ ng test
 10% building modules 1/1 modules 0 active04 07 2017 19:50:33.319:WARN [karma]: No captured browser,
 open http://localhost:9876/
04 07 2017 19:50:33.327:INFO [karma]: Karma v1.7.0 server started at http://0.0.0.0:9876/
04 07 2017 19:50:33.328:INFO [launcher]: Launching browser Chrome with unlimited concurrency
04 07 2017 19:50:33.333:INFO [launcher]: Starting browser Chrome
04 07 2017 19:50:38.395:WARN [karma]: No captured browser, open http://localhost:9876/
04 07 2017 19:50:38.517:INFO [Chrome 59.0.3071 (Mac OS X 10.12.4)]: Connected on socket tXgGCkUlAt2E
dsg4AAAA with id 17471874
Chrome 59.0.3071 (Mac OS X 10.12.4): Executed 4 of 4 SUCCESS (0.228 secs / 0.213 secs)
```

You may be wondering why the last line says 4 tests instead of 3; remember that the quote component we generated had a single test suite as well.

Summary

In this chapter, you learned how to create Angular projects and what files necessarily accompany a new project. Now you know how to create Angular projects, and scaffold building blocks such as components, and understand the basic skeleton of components. You also learned why modules exist, how to apply simple styles to components, and what unit tests look like in Angular.

In the next chapter, we will delve into the creation of more components and see some examples in play.

5
Advanced Custom Components with TypeScript

In the previous chapter, we discussed the basics of component creation and usage. This knowledge is not enough to build robust applications. We need to delve a little more deeply into Angular's exciting components and see how TypeScript makes working with components a lot easier.

We are going to address the following topics while showing some hands-on examples on how they work:

- **Lifecycle hooks**: These are class methods in Angular that you can hook into. They are achievable by implementing a TypeScript interface.
- **ElementRef**: This involves manipulating and querying DOM safely in Angular using the ElementRef API.
- **View encapsulation**: You will learn how scoped styles are applied to Angular components and how to change the default behavior.

Lifecycle hooks

Most methods you will create in classes must be called somewhere by you, which is the expected pattern in programming. This is not the case in what Angular defines as lifecycle hooks. These hooks are methods that you create for Angular to call them internally, depending on the current state of a component/directive. They are created in a component's or directive's class.

The following hooks are available in an Angular component:

- ngOnChanges: Remember how properties are bound to components. These properties are reactive, meaning that, when they change, the view is updated as well. This lifecycle method is called when any property, bound to a view, is changed. Therefore, you can manipulate what happens before the changes are reflected.
- ngOnInit: This is the most common lifecycle. It is called after a component has been initialized with the default property bindings. Hence, it is called after the first ngOnChanges.
- ngDoCheck: Reactivity (change detection) is usually handled for you, but in extreme cases where it's not, you need to handle it yourself. Use ngDoCheck to detect and act upon changes that Angular can't or won't detect on its own.
- ngAfterContentInit: This is called after the component's content has been initialized.
- ngAfterContentChecked: This is called after every check on the component's content.
- ngAfterViewInit: This is called after initializing the view based on the component's template.
- ngAfterViewChecked: This is called after checking a component's view and the child views of a component.
- ngOnDestroy: This is called before a component is destroyed. This is a good place for a clean-up.

Some lifecycle hooks may not make sense immediately. You shouldn't worry about them because it's only in extreme cases that you will need a lot of them.

An example will help clarify how they work. Let's explore the most common hook, which is ngOnInit.

Create a new Angular project with the CLI command. Open the app component TypeScript file and update the imports to include OnInit:

```
// Code: 5.1
//./src/app/app.component.ts

import { Component, OnInit } from '@angular/core';
```

OnInit is an interface that any class intended to implement ngOnInit should inherit. This is not technically required (see https://angular.io/guide/lifecycle-hooks#interfaces-are-optional-technically).

You can now make the AppComponent class implement this interface:

```
// Code: 5.1
//./src/app/app.component.ts

@Component({
  selector: 'app-root',
  templateUrl: './app.component.html',
  styleUrls: ['./app.component.css']
})
export class AppComponent implements OnInit {
  title: string = 'Items in Bag';
  items: Array<string> = [];
  loading: boolean = false;
  ngOnInit () {
    this.loading = true;
    setTimeout(() => {
      this.items = [
          'Pen',
          'Note',
          'Mug',
          'Charger',
          'Passport',
          'Keys'
      ]
      this.loading = false;
    }, 3000)
  }
}
```

We are trying to simulate an asynchronous behavior, where values are resolved in the future. This kind of operation is best done when the application is initialized and that's why we are handling this in the ngOnInit method. Once the component is ready, Angular calls this hook, which will set the item array after three seconds.

We can bind the values to the view even before they come in. Angular will always update the view when the values are available:

```html
<!-- Code: 5.1 -->
<!-- ./src/app/app.component.html -->

<div style="text-align:center">
  <h1>  {{title}}!!  </h1>
  <h4 *ngIf="loading">Please wait...</h4>
</div>
<ul>
  <li *ngFor="let item of items">{{item}}</li>
</ul>
```

To iterate over a list in Angular templates, we use the *ngFor **structural directive**, as shown in the preceding example. The *ngIf structural directive is like *ngFor but is used to display DOM elements based on a Boolean property on the component.

As usual, run the app with ng serve, and you will see the following first:

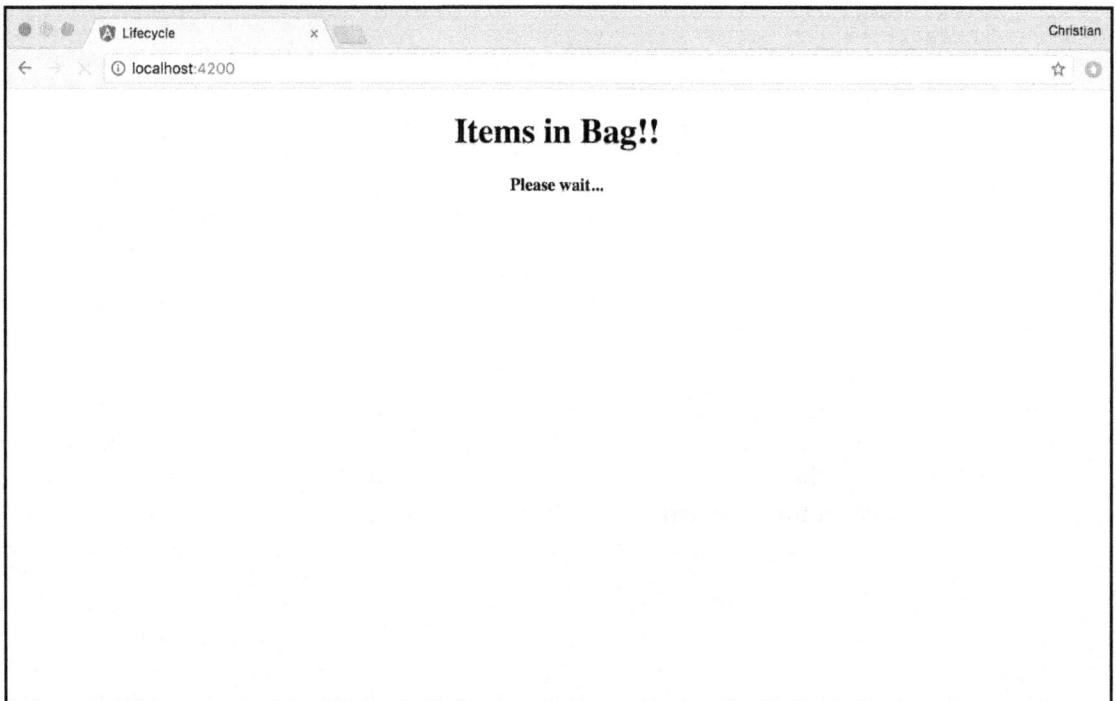

After three seconds, the **Please wait...** text will disappear, and you will see your list of items:

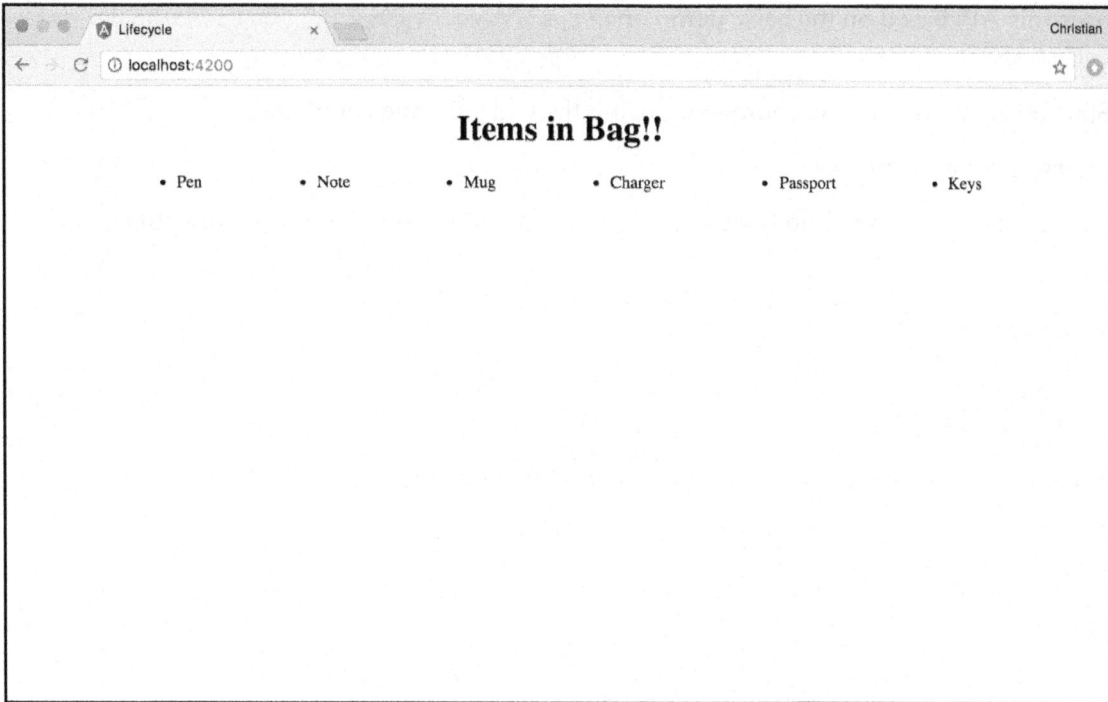

DOM manipulation

In Angular 1.x, touching the DOM seemed mysterious; not like you couldn't, but somehow it comes back to bite you. This is ironic because what we do as web designers/developers is paint the DOM, and that cannot be possible without manipulating it.

With Angular 2+, it became quite easy to do this. Angular abstracts the DOM and gives you the shallow copy to mess around with. It's then responsible for putting it back without hurting anyone. It becomes even more interesting with TypeScript because your editor can hint most of the DOM property methods for you.

ElementRef

The API to achieve Dom manipulation is `ElementRef`. Let's build a tab component that uses this API based on the basic demo on `https://www.w3schools.com/howto/howto_js_tabs.asp`.

Start by generating a new component using the CLI generate command:

```
ng g component tab
```

Add the template as a child to our app component right after the `*ngFor` directive:

```html
<ul>
  <li *ngFor="let item of items">{{item}}</li>
</ul>

<!--Add tab component to app-->
<app-tab></app-tab>
```

Then, replace the component's template with the following:

```html
<!--./src/app/tab/tab.component.css-->
<div class="tab">
  <button class="tablink" (click)="openTab($event,
'London')">London</button>
  <button class="tablink" (click)="openTab($event, 'Paris')">Paris</button>
  <button class="tablink" (click)="openTab($event, 'Tokyo')">Tokyo</button>
</div>

<div id="London" class="tabcontent">
  <h3>London</h3>
  <p>London is the capital city of England.</p>
</div>
<div id="Paris" class="tabcontent">
  <h3>Paris</h3>
  <p>Paris is the capital of France.</p>
</div>
<div id="Tokyo" class="tabcontent">
  <h3>Tokyo</h3>
  <p>Tokyo is the capital of Japan.</p>
</div>
```

You should see the result on the browser, as shown in the following screenshot:

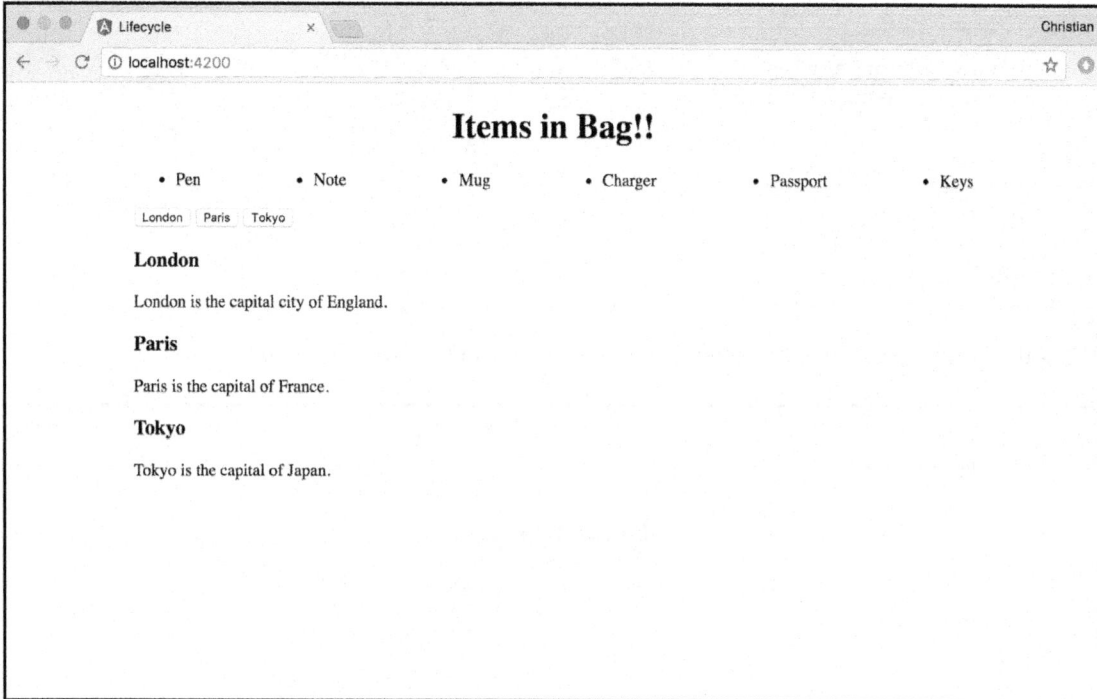

Let's add some styles to create a tabbed look:

```
// based on styles from the base sample

/* ./src/app/tab/tab.component.css */
div.tab {
  overflow: hidden;
  border: 1px solid #ccc;
  background-color: #f1f1f1;
 }

div.tab button {
  background-color: inherit;
  float: left;
  border: none;
  outline: none;
  cursor: pointer;
  padding: 14px 16px;
  transition: 0.3s;
 }
```

```
div.tab button:hover {
  background-color: #ddd;
 }

div.tab button.active {
  background-color: #ccc;
 }

.tabcontent {
  padding: 6px 12px;
  border: 1px solid #ccc;
  border-top: none;
}
```

With the styles, you should have the result shown in the following screenshot:

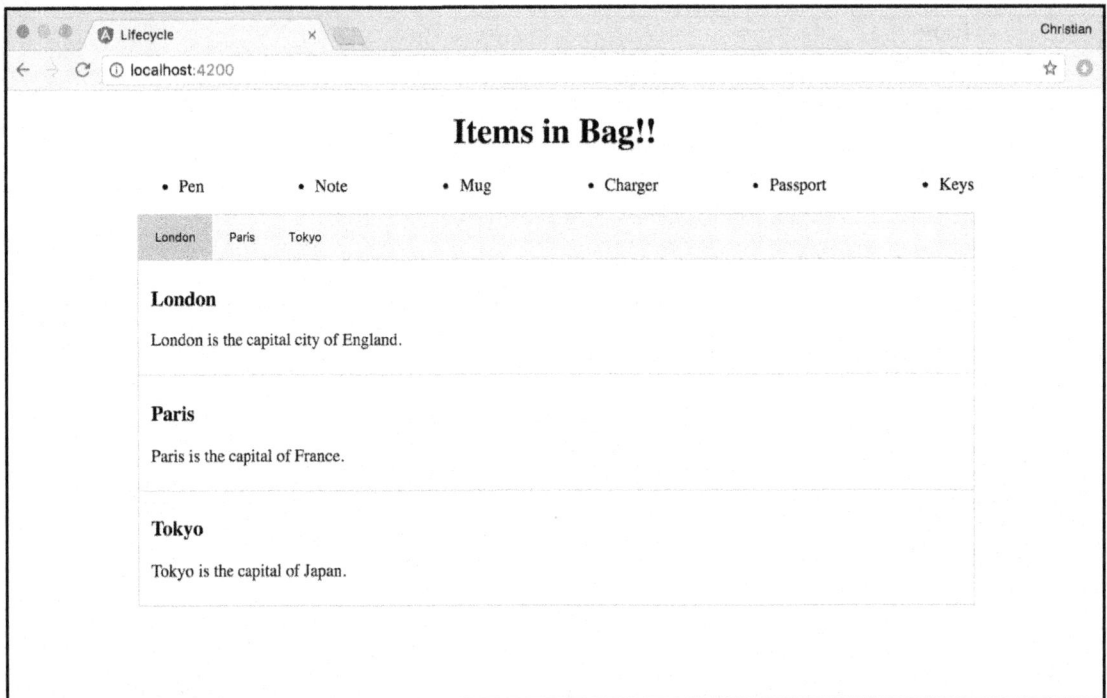

Now is the time to start manipulating the DOM. We first need to hide all the tab contents with CSS by default; then, they can be activated in TypeScript:

```
.tabcontent {
  display: none;
  }
```

Hooking into content initialization

To be assured of gaining access to the DOM, we need to hook into the ngAfterContentInit lifecycle method. It's in this method that we can use ElementRef to query the DOM and manipulate it:

```
import { Component, ElementRef, OnInit, AfterContentInit } from
'@angular/core';

@Component({
  selector: 'app-tab',
  templateUrl: './tab.component.html',
  styleUrls: ['./tab.component.css']
  })

export class TabComponent implements OnInit, AfterContentInit {
  tabContents: Array<HTMLElement>;
  tabLinks: Array<HTMLElement>;
  constructor(
    private el: ElementRef
  ) { }

  ngOnInit() {}

  ngAfterContentInit() {
    // Grab the DOM
    this.tabContents =
this.el.nativeElement.querySelectorAll('.tabcontent');
    this.tabLinks = this.el.nativeElement.querySelectorAll('.tablink');
    }
}
```

The class implements `AfterContentInit` as well as `OnInint`, showing how you can implement multiple interfaces. Then, we declare the buttons as an array of `HTMLElement` links. This also applies to the tab contents.

Right in the constructor, we create an instance of `ElementRef` as `el`, which we can use to interact with the DOM. The `ngAfterContentInit` function is called after the DOM contents are ready, which makes it the perfect candidate to handle DOM manipulations on startup. Hence, we grab a reference to the DOM there.

We need to show the first tab and make the first tab link active on load. Let's extend `ngAfterContentInit` to achieve this:

```
export class TabComponent implements OnInit, AfterContentInit {
  tabContents: Array<HTMLElement>;
  tabLinks: Array<HTMLElement>;
  constructor(
    private el: ElementRef
  ) { }
  ngOnInit() {}
  ngAfterContentInit() {
    this.tabContents =
this.el.nativeElement.querySelectorAll('.tabcontent');
    this.tabLinks = this.el.nativeElement.querySelectorAll('.tablink');
    // Activate first tab
    this.tabContents[0].style.display = "block";
    this.tabLinks[0].className = " active";
  }
}
```

This will display the first tab, as shown in the following screenshot:

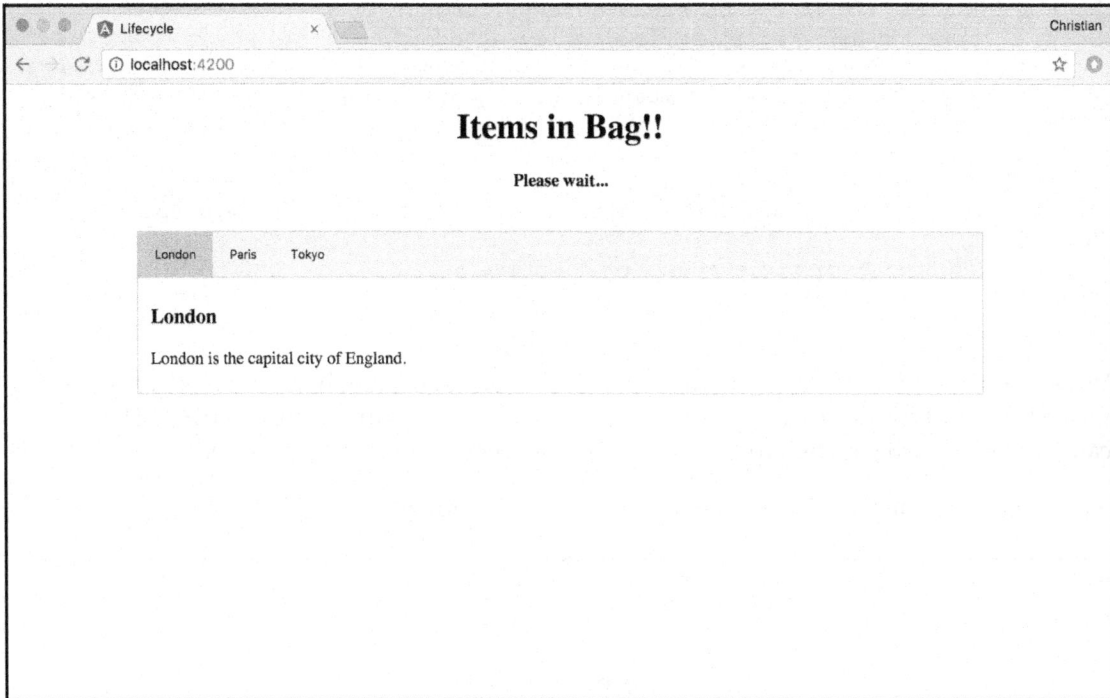

Handling DOM events

The final thing to do is add event listeners to the click events and start switching tabs. In the preceding template, we have click events attached to each button:

```
<button class="tablink" (click)="open($event, 'London')">London</button>
<button class="tablink" (click)="open($event, 'Paris')">Paris</button>
<button class="tablink" (click)="open($event, 'Tokyo')">Tokyo</button>
```

The `openTab` method is the event handler. Let's implement it:

```
export class TabComponent implements OnInit, AfterContentInit {
  tabContents: Array<HTMLElement>;
 tabLinks: Array<HTMLElement>;
  constructor(
 private el: ElementRef
  ) { }
  // ...
```

```
open(evt, cityName) {
    for (let i = 0; i < this.tabContents.length; i++) {
      this.tabContents[i].style.display = "none";
    }
    for (let i = 0; i < this.tabLinks.length; i++) {
      this.tabLinks[i].className = this.tabLinks[i].className.replace("
active", "");
    }
    this.el.nativeElement.querySelector(`#${cityName}`).style.display =
"block";
    evt.currentTarget.className += " active";
  }
}
```

When the method is called, we iterate over all the tabs and hide them. We also iterate over the buttons and disable them by replacing the active class with an empty string. Then, we can display the tab we want to open and activate the button that was clicked.

Now when you click tab buttons, each tab content is shown:

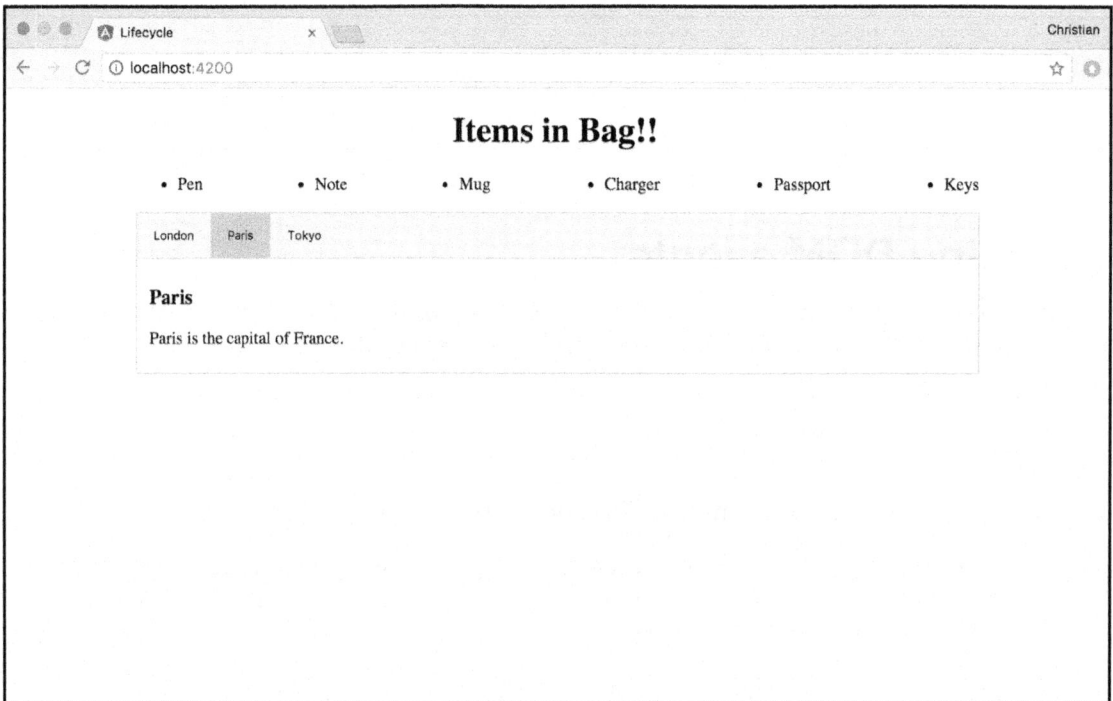

There are different ways to solve this, and some of them are more advanced. The example we just showed intentionally performs DOM querying to show you how possible and simple it is to do DOM manipulation in Angular.

View encapsulation

Components can be configured to apply styles differently. This concept is called encapsulation, and that's what we are going to discuss now.

Create another project with the CLI and add an extra component with the following command:

```
ng g component child
```

Then, add this new component to the view via the app component:

```
// Code 5.2
<!-- ./src/app/app.component.html -->

<div style="text-align:center">
  <h1>  This is parent component  </h1>
  <app-child></app-child>
</div>
```

The child component's template is as simple as this:

```
// Code 5.2
<!-- ./src/app/child/child.component.html -->

<h3>This is child component </h3>
```

That's just the minimum setup we need in order to understand view encapsulation strategies. Let's explore them.

Emulated

This is the default strategy. Any style applied globally via HTML (not the parent component) as well as all the styles applied to a component will be reflected. In our case, if we target h3 and apply styles to `style.css`, `app.component.css`, and `child.component.css`, only `style.css` and `child.component.css` will be reflected.

The following CSS is the child component:

```
h3 {  color: palevioletred }
```

On running the preceding code, the result on the child component's view is as follows:

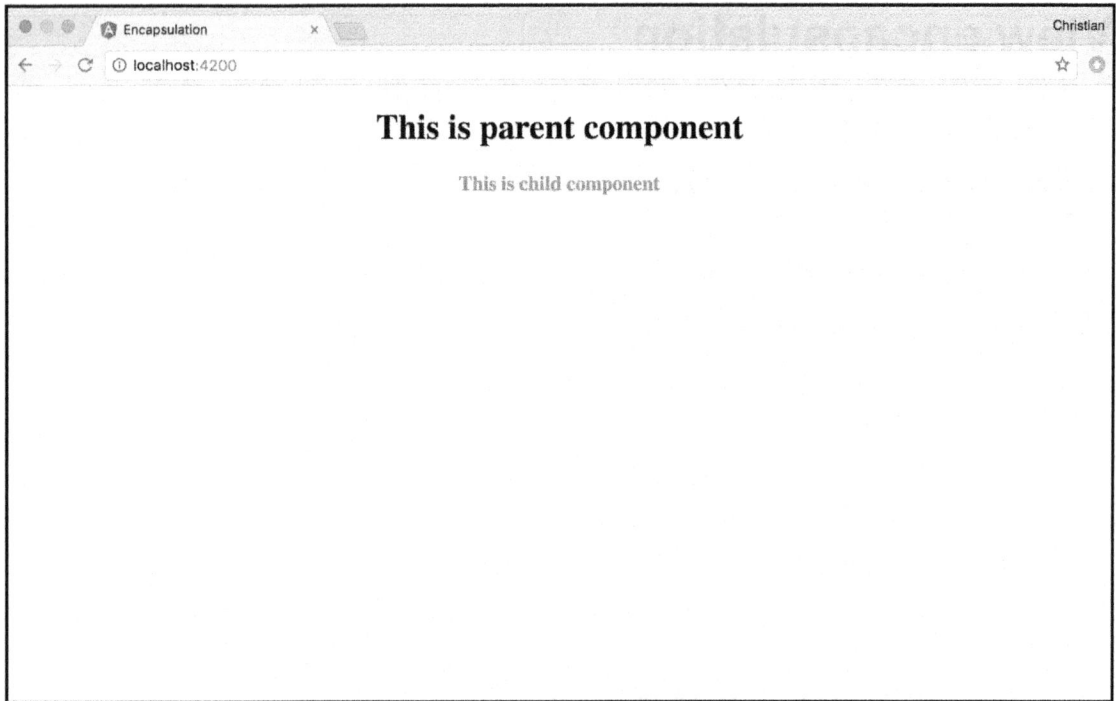

In cases where the same styles are applied to the same element on both the global styles and the component itself, the component styles supersede the global style. For example, consider that the `style.css` file is as follows:

```
h3 {
  color: palevioletred
}
```

Now consider that the `child.component.css` file is as follows:

```
h3 {
  color: blueviolet
}
```

The color of h3 will be blueviolet, as shown in the following screenshot:

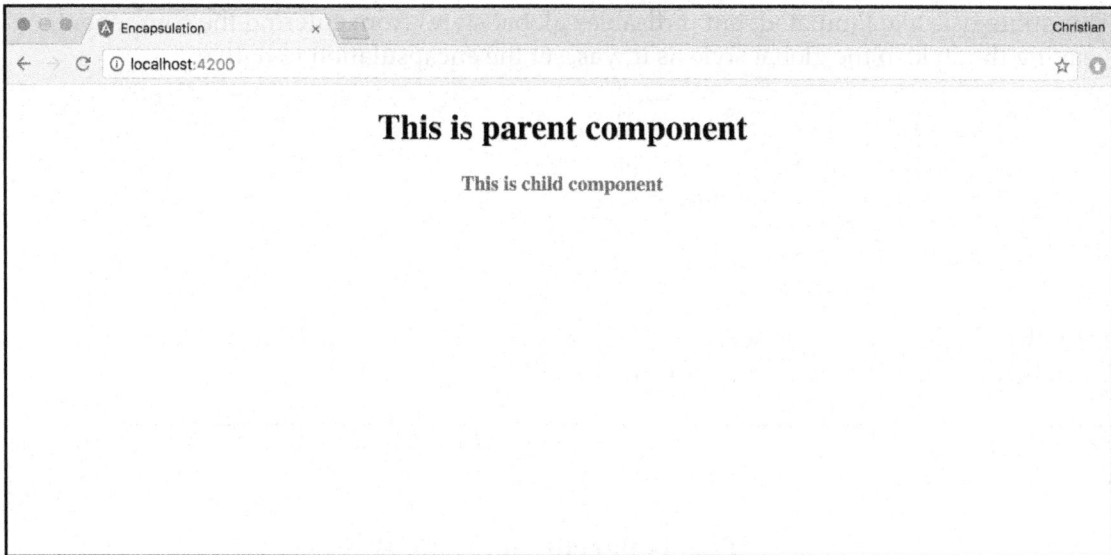

You can set this in the component decorator, though it is not necessary because Emulated is the default value:

```
import { Component, OnInit, ViewEncapsulation } from '@angular/core';

@Component({
  selector: 'app-child',
</span>  templateUrl: './child.component.html',
  styleUrls: ['./child.component.css'],
  // Encapsulation: Emulated
  encapsulation: ViewEncapsulation.Emulated
})

export class ChildComponent implements OnInit {
  constructor() { }
  ngOnInit() {  }
}
```

Native

This strategy is like Emulated, but it disables global styles from entering the component. Leaving the style in the global style as it was, set the encapsulation to native:

```
@Component({
  selector: 'app-child',
  templateUrl: './child.component.html',
  styleUrls: ['./child.component.css'],
 // Encapsulation: Native
  encapsulation: ViewEncapsulation.Native
})
```

Even though the global style sets the h3 color to pinkvioletred, the text color remains black because it couldn't penetrate the template:

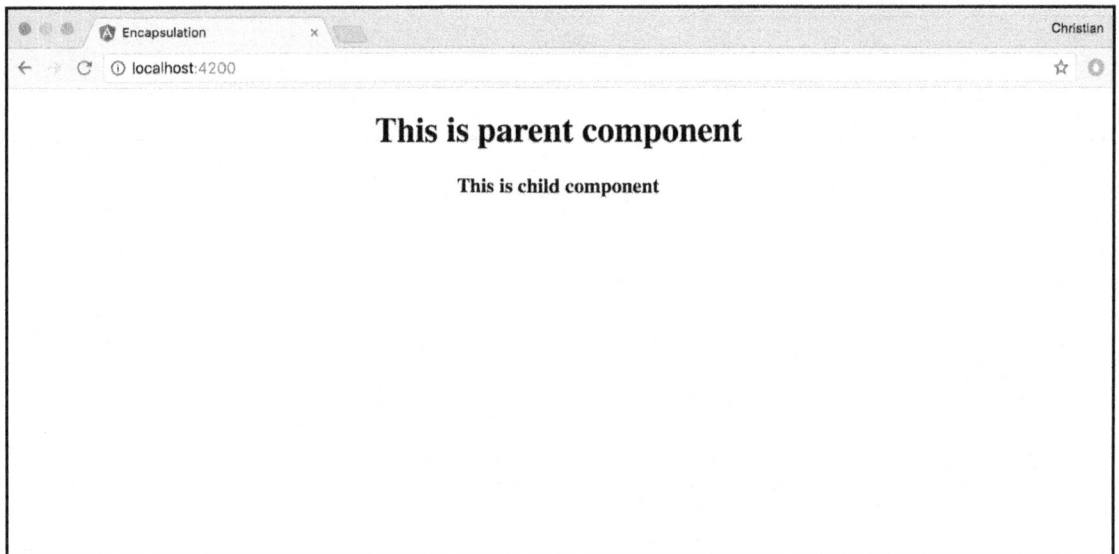

None

This is the freest strategy. No matter where the style is set--child or parent--the styles are leaked to the other components:

```
@Component({
  selector: 'app-child',
  templateUrl: './child.component.html',
  styleUrls: ['./child.component.css'],
 // Encapsulation: Native
  encapsulation: ViewEncapsulation.None
})
```

With this setting, you can style the h1 tag in the parent tag via the child component's styles:

```
// child component style
h1 {
  color: blueviolet
}
```

This reflects in the view, as shown in the following image:

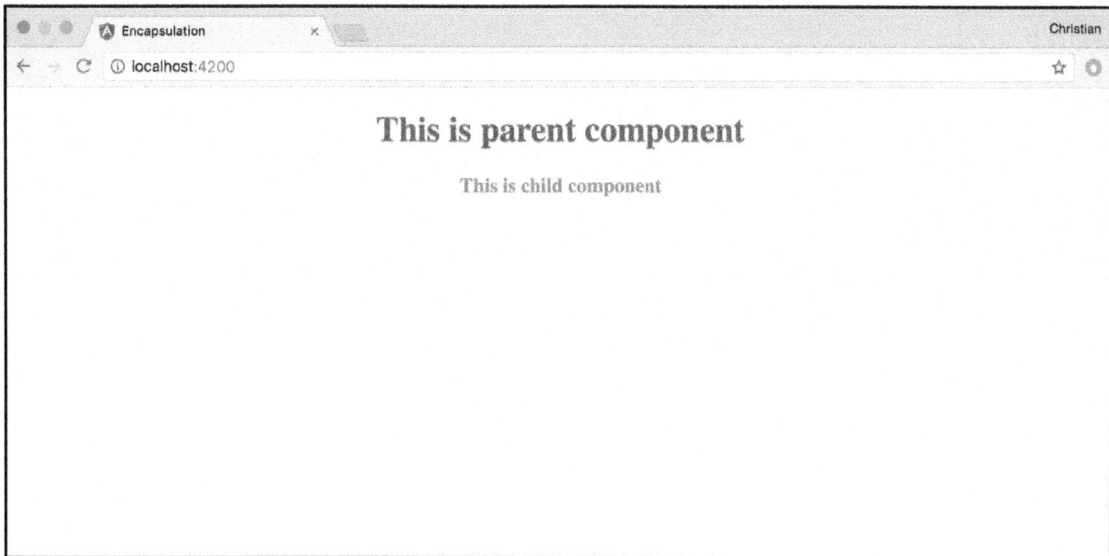

Summary

Hopefully, the advanced topics discussed were not so complex or difficult to comprehend. You learned how to implement lifecycle hooks, control the behavior of component-scoped styles, and manipulate the DOM content after it has been rendered.

If you take only one thing from this chapter, let it be how to implement the lifecycle interfaces with TypeScript and using TypeScript decorators to configure a component. In the next chapter, you will learn about component communication and how components interact with each other via properties, events, view children, and content children.

6
Component Composition with TypeScript

The components you write with TypeScript are at their best when kept short and simple. However, a short and simple component will hardly make a full-blown app. How do you compose components performing specific tasks and combine them to make a usable application? This is what this chapter is all about. We will discuss the following topics:

- Component hierarchy
- Communication between components at different levels

We will also see some hands-on examples on how components are composed and how these composed components communicate with each other.

Component composability

Composability is the most outstanding feature and the selling point of components. As a matter of fact, this is what makes components what they are. Not just on the web but whenever an entity is referred to as a component, then it has a tendency to be composed with other components.

While some components can function on their own, most depend implicitly or explicitly on other stand-alone components to achieve a given task. TypeScript and templates greatly simplify composition in Angular, enabling it to put the pieces of our app together in a seamless and an easy-to-maintain way.

Composition happens hierarchically; hence, most component relationships are either parent-to-child or child-to-parent. It is also important to keep in mind that if such a parent-child relationship exists, then some components might be siblings to others, depending on the architecture.

Hierarchical composition

A composed component has a parental relationship with another component, either as the parent or as a child. There is a tendency for a nested chain; hence, nothing stops a child component from having a grandparent or a parent component from having a grandchild component.

The following screenshot illustrates this better:

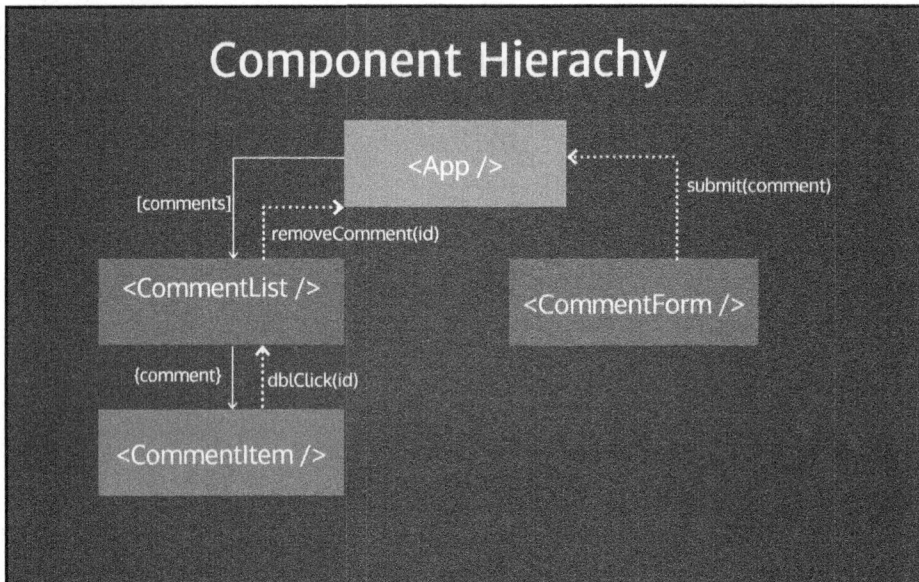

Here, the entry App component has two child components: CommentList and CommentForm. CommentList also has a child, CommentItem. It's okay to say that CommentItem is the grandchild of App. It's also okay to say that CommentList and CommentForm are siblings.

The thick arrows show how the data flows from the parent components down to the child components, while the dotted arrows show how the data is pushed as events from the child components to the parent components. This illustration of data flowing down and moving up leads us to our next topic for discussion: component communication.

Component communication

Based on the diagram that we saw previously, let's see some examples in action. The recommended place to start is the data flow from parent to child.

Parent-child flow

Jump right in and create a new Angular project using the Angular CLI. With that done, update AppComponent with the following content:

```
import { Component } from '@angular/core';

@Component({
  selector: 'app-root',
  templateUrl: './app.component.html',
  styleUrls: ['./app.component.css']
})
export class AppComponent {
  title = 'app';
  comments = [
    {
      author: 'Jay Kay',
      content: 'TypeScript makes Angular awesome'
    },
    {
      author: 'William',
      content: 'Yeah, right!'
    },
    {
      author: 'Raphael',
      content: 'Got stuck passing data around'
    }
  ]
}
```

The key difference is that I have added an array of comments. These comments are what we intend to pass down to the child component.

Let's create `CommentListComponent` using the Angular CLI generate command:

```
ng g component comment-list
```

The created component is meant to receive a list of comments from the parent component, `AppComponent`. When it receives this component, it can iterate over them and print them on the screen:

```
import { Component, OnInit, Input } from '@angular/core';

@Component({
  selector: 'app-comment-list',
  templateUrl: './comment-list.component.html',
  styleUrls: ['./comment-list.component.css']
})
export class CommentListComponent implements OnInit {

  // Received via Imputs
  @Input() comments;

  constructor() { }
  ngOnInit() {}

}
```

The `Input` TypeScript decorator is used to specify that a class property will be set by a parent component. Hence, we do not need to set any values on `CommentListComponent.comments`, but we need to wait until a value is passed down to it via `AppComponent`. Remember `AppComponent.comments` exists as well, so we can use property binding to pass `AppComponent.comments` to `CommentListComponent.comments` in `app.component.html`:

```
<div>
  <h2>Comments</h2>
  <app-comment-list [comments]="comments"></app-comment-list>
</div>
```

The `comments` array is the value passed to the `[comments]` attribute. This attribute is what we created and decorated in the `CommentListComponent` component.

Now you have an array of comments on the parent component (AppComponent); you have passed this component down to the child component (CommentListComponent) via property binding, and you're receiving the list of comments using the Input decorator. The next thing you need to do is display the received comments on comment-list.component.html:

```html
<div class="comment-box" *ngFor="let comment of comments">
  <h3>{{comment.author}}</h3>
  <p>{{comment.content}}</p>
</div>
```

The *ngFor directive is used to iterate over the comments, get each comment, and display a comment on our view.

This is what the output looks like:

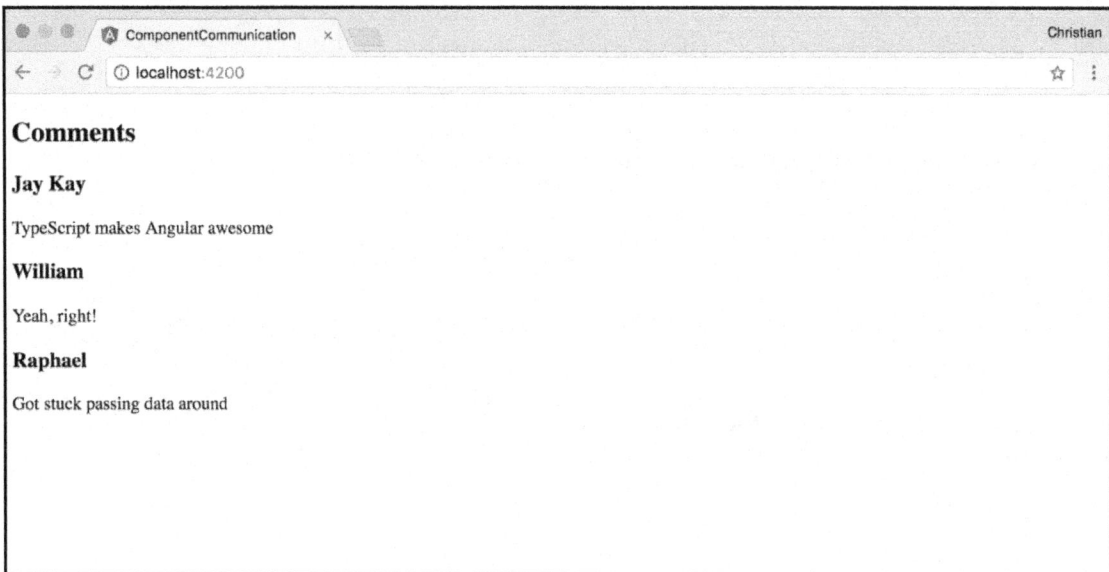

You can go a level deeper to create a comment item component, which just takes a single comment and displays it. Create another component:

```
ng g component comment-item
```

Add a decorated comment property, which will receive the comment item from the comment list:

```
import { Component, OnInit, Input } from '@angular/core';

@Component({
  selector: 'app-comment-item',
  templateUrl: './comment-item.component.html',
  styleUrls: ['./comment-item.component.css']
})
export class CommentItemComponent implements OnInit {

  // Decorated comment
  @Input() comment;

  constructor() { }

  ngOnInit() {}

}
```

Send the comment down via the `comment list` parent component:

```
<app-comment-item
  *ngFor="let comment of comments" [comment]="comment">
</app-comment-item>
```

The `comment` template variable doesn't have to exist on the component class. It's procured from the iterator.

Then, you can simply render the comment item on the `comment-item.component.html` template:

```
<h3>{{comment.author}}</h3>
<p>{{comment.content}}</p>
```

Adding another child illustrates nesting. `App | comment list | comment item` is the flow. `App` is the parent of `comment list` and the grandparent of `comment item`. `comment list` is the parent of `comment item`.

Head to the browser and see that, while nothing actually changes, our code is structured better:

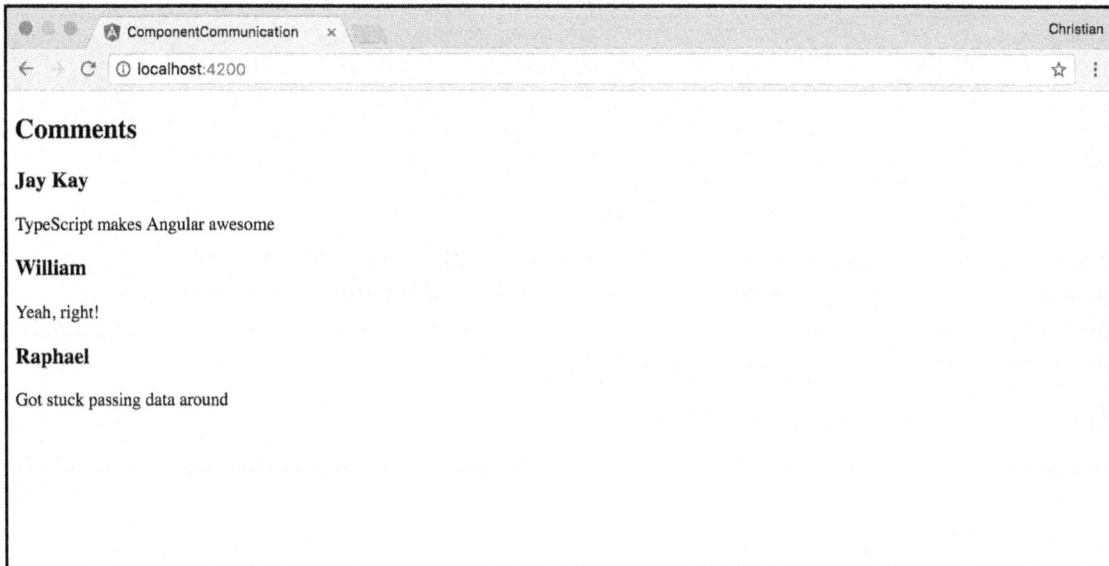

Intercepting property changes

Sometimes, you may want to do some tweaking on the data flowing into a child component from the parent component. You can use getters and setters to intercept the data and manipulate it before setting it on the view. Let's see that in play by capitalizing the author names before they are set:

```
import { Component, OnInit, Input } from '@angular/core';

@Component({
  selector: 'app-comment-item',
  templateUrl: './comment-item.component.html',
  styleUrls: ['./comment-item.component.css']
})
export class CommentItemComponent implements OnInit {
  private _comment;
  constructor() { }

  ngOnInit() {}

  @Input()
  set comment(comment) {
```

```
      this._comment = Object.assign(comment, {
         author: comment.author.toUpperCase()
      });
   }

   get comment() {
      return this._comment
   }

}
```

The decorator is no longer set on the value property but on the setter property. This property receives the comment from the comment list—the parent component. It then overrides the author property with an uppercase version of the author's name. The getter just returns the comment, so you can access it from the view.

The following is how it looks in the browser:

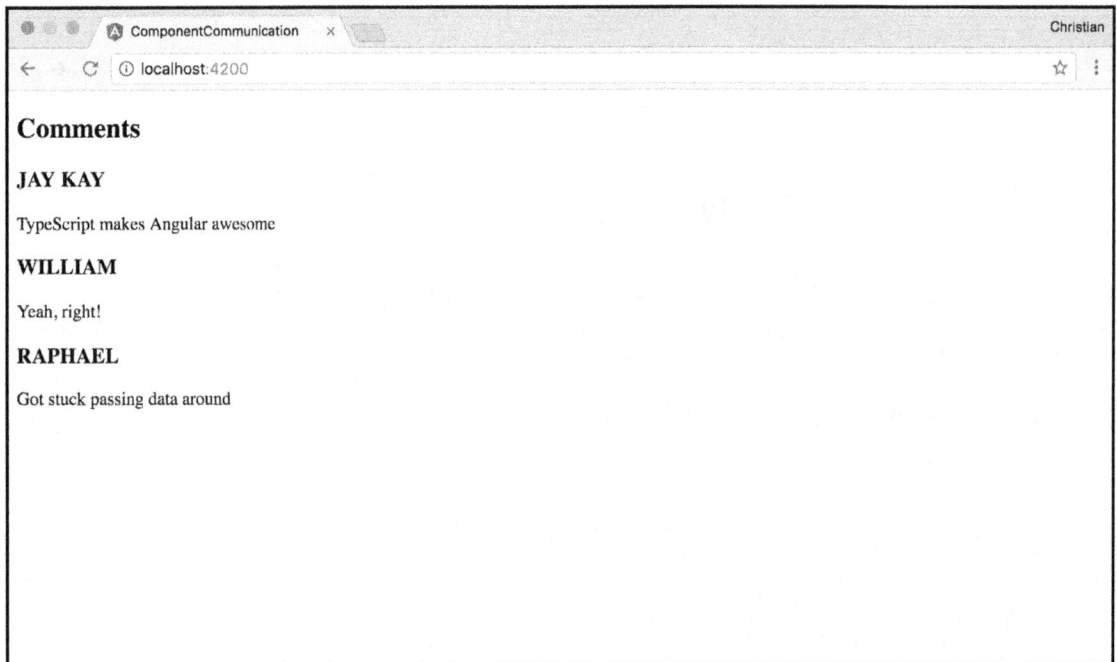

Child–parent flow

In this flow, rather than passing data down, the data needs to flow up the chain. Most of the time, the data flows up based on the events triggered on the child by the user and we try to notify the parent about that event. Hence, Angular allows you to listen to the child events on the parent component and to act on the events. These events can be characterized with the data as the payload.

Let's start by registering a double-click event on each comment item via the comment list component:

```
<app-comment-item
  *ngFor="let comment of comments"
  [comment]="comment"
  (dblclick)="showComment(comment)">
</app-comment-item>
```

Then, you need to add the `showComment` handler on the component class to handle this event:

```
import {
  Component,
  OnInit,
  Input,
  EventEmitter,
  Output } from '@angular/core';

@Component({
  selector: 'app-comment-list',
  templateUrl: './comment-list.component.html',
  styleUrls: ['./comment-list.component.css']
})
export class CommentListComponent implements OnInit {

  @Input() comments;
  @Output() onShowComment = new EventEmitter();

  constructor() { }
  ngOnInit() {}

  showComment(comment) {
    this.onShowComment.emit(comment);
  }

}
```

The handler uses `onShowComment`, which is decorated as an output property with the `Output` decorator to emit an event of the `EventEmitter` type. This emitted event is what the parent component will need to listen to. Note how the comment is passed to the `emit` method; this shows how we can pass data from the child to the parent.

Next, we listen to the parent component (`App`) for this event to occur:

```
<div>
  <h2>Comments</h2>
  <app-comment-list
    [comments]="comments"
    (onShowComment)="onShowComment($event)">
  </app-comment-list>
</div>
```

Note that the event binding annotation, `()`, is used for events, in this case, `onShowComment`. The binding refers to `EventEmitter`, while its value refers to the handler method that is yet to be created. The handler method is called, and we pass the value data from the child component as `$event`.

Here is the implementation of the handler:

```
import { Component } from '@angular/core';

@Component({
  selector: 'app-root',
  templateUrl: './app.component.html',
  styleUrls: ['./app.component.css']
})
export class AppComponent {
  title = 'app';
  comments = [
    {
      author: 'Jay Kay',
      content: 'TypeScript makes Angular awesome'
    },
    // ...
  ]

  onShowComment(comment) {
    alert(comment.content);
  }
}
```

The method just alerts the comment as shown in the following screenshot:

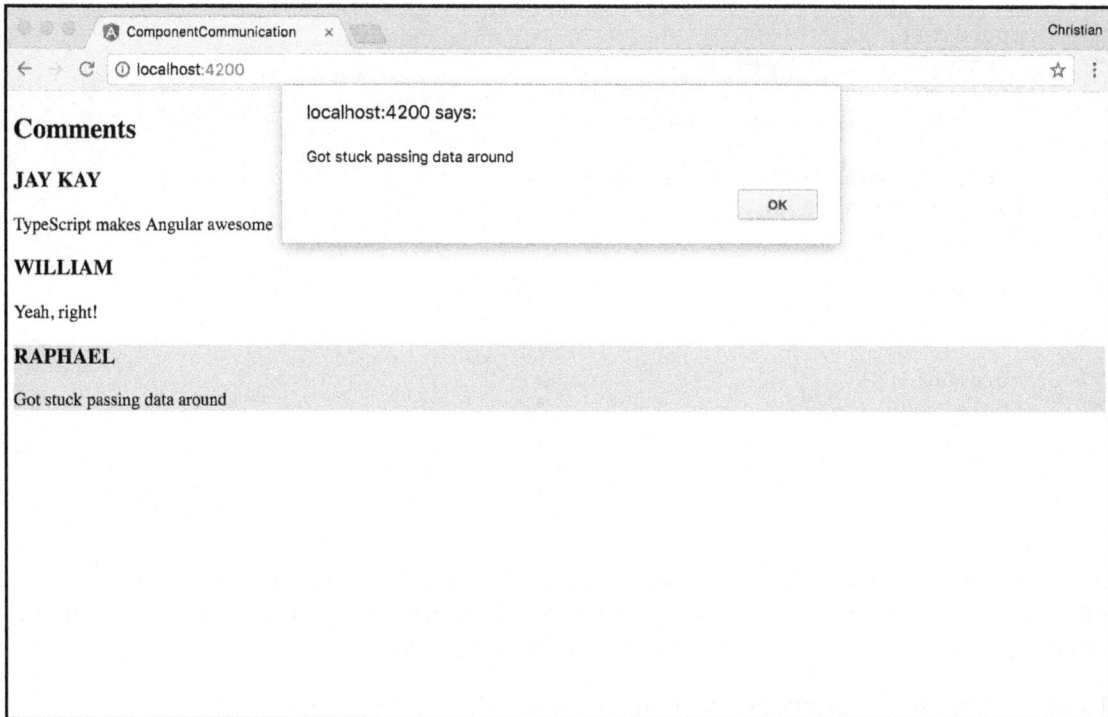

Accessing properties and methods of a child via a parent component

Other than data flowing in and the event pushed up, there are other strategies for communication. We can access child members from the parent component using template variables. Let's create a counter component to serve as our example:

```
ng g component counter
```

Now add a counter variable and initialize it to zero:

```
//counter.component.html
<h5>
  {{counter}}
</h5>
```

```
//counter.component.ts
import { Component, OnInit } from '@angular/core';

@Component({
  selector: 'app-counter',
  templateUrl: './counter.component.html',
  styleUrls: ['./counter.component.css']
})
export class CounterComponent implements OnInit {
  counter: number = 0;

  increment() {
    this.counter++
  }

  decrement() {
    this.counter--
  }

}
```

Also, there are two methods to just increment or decrement the counter. Note that nothing calls these methods; there are no buttons with an event attached to increment or decrement. What we want to do is access these methods from the parent component.

To do so, add the component to the template with a template variable:

```
<div>
  <h2>Comments</h2>
  <app-comment-list [comments]="comments"
(onShowComment)="onShowComment($event)"></app-comment-list>

  ...

  <h2>Counter</h2>
  <app-counter #counter></app-counter>

</div>
```

#counter is a variable that is accessible from anywhere in the template. Hence, you can use it as an object to access the methods and properties of the counter component:

```
<div>
  <h2>Comments</h2>
  <app-comment-list [comments]="comments"
(onShowComment)="onShowComment($event)"></app-comment-list>
```

```
    ...
    <h2>Counter</h2>
    <app-counter #counter></app-counter>
    <button (click)="counter.increment()">++</button>
    <button (click)="counter.decrement()">--</button>
</div>
```

This shows a button counter with buttons that we can click to increment or decrement the counter:

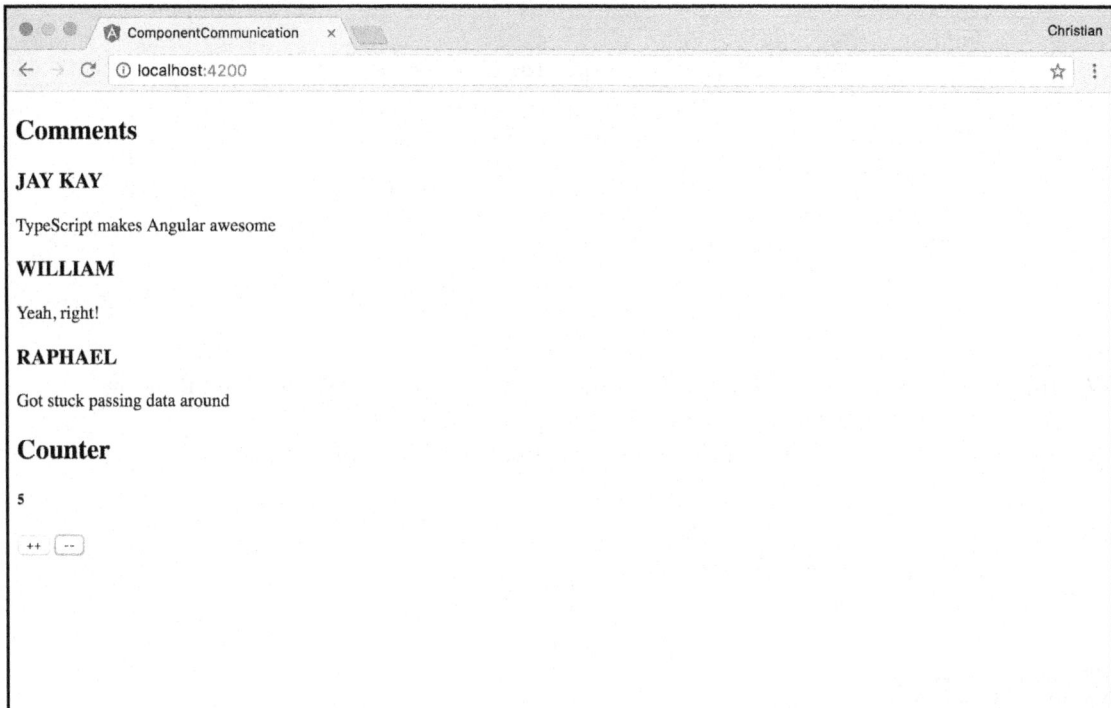

Accessing child members with ViewChild

If the template variables don't feel natural, you can achieve the same behavior using `ViewChild`. This allows you to access the child as a variable on the class and not on the template:

```
//app.component.ts
import { Component, ViewChild } from '@angular/core';
import { CounterComponent } from './counter/counter.component'
```

```
@Component({
  selector: 'app-root',
  templateUrl: './app.component.html',
  styleUrls: ['./app.component.css']
})
export class AppComponent {
  @ViewChild(CounterComponent)
  counterComponent: CounterComponent

  comments = [
    {</span&gt;
      author: 'Jay Kay',
      content: 'TypeScript makes Angular awesome'
    },
    // ...
  ]

  onShowComment(comment) {
    alert(comment.content);
  }
}
```

We import the counter component and register it as a child of this component using `ViewChild`. We then create a `counterComponent` variable of the `CounterComponent` type. We can then use this variable in our template:

```
<app-counter></app-counter>
<button (click)="counterComponent.increment()">++</button>
<button (click)="counterComponent.decrement()">--</button>
```

Summary

Now you can start using components as building blocks by writing small, maintainable components and making them interact with each other using composition. In this chapter, you learned what hierarchical inheritance means in component architectures, how data flows up and down hierarchical trees, and how components interact with each other.

In the next chapter, we will explore a more centric interaction strategy using services. This will help us create logic that components will share, hence keeping our codebase very DRY (Don't Reapeat Yourself).

7
Separating Concerns with Typed Services

This chapter builds on the previous chapter, with more techniques showing how communication occurs within your application's building blocks. You will learn the following topics in this chapter:

- Services and Dependency Injection (DI) concepts
- Component communication with services
- Writing data logic with services

To understand services better, you need to understand at least the basic concepts of Dependency Injection.

Dependency injection

Writing Angular in TypeScript demands that your building blocks (components, directives, services, and so on) are written in classes. They are just building blocks, which means that they need to be intertwined with each other before they can become functional, thus making a full-blown application.

This intertwining process can be pretty daunting. For this reason, let's understand the problem first. Take the following TypeScript class, for instance:

```
export class Developer {
  private skills: Array<Skill>;
  private bio: Person;
  constructor() {
    this.bio = new Person('Sarah', 'Doe', 24, 'female');
```

```
    this.skills = [
      new Skill('css'),
      new Skill('TypeScript'),
      new Skill('Webpack')
    ];
  }
}
```

The implementation of the `Person` and `Skill` classes is as simple as the following:

```
// Person Class
export class Person {
  private fName: string;
  private lName: string;
  private age: number;
  private gender: string;
  constructor(
    fName: string,
    lName: string,
    age: number,
    gender: string,
  ) {
    this.fName = fName;
    this.lName = lName;
    this.age = age;
    this.gender = gender;
  }
}

// Skill Class
export class Skill {
  private type: string;
  constructor(
    type: string
  ) {
    this.type = type;
  }
}
```

The preceding sample is very functional and valid code until you starting having more developer types that need to be created using this class. There is no way to actually create another type of developer because all the implementation details are tied to a class; hence, the process isn't flexible. We need to make the class a lot more generic before it can be used to create more types of developer.

Let's try improving the `Developer` class, so it receives all the values needed to create a class from the constructor rather than setting it in the class:

```
export class Developer {
  private skills: Array<Skills>;
  private bio: Person;
  constructor(
    fName: string,
    lName: string,
    age: number,
    gender: string,
    skills: Array<string>
  ) {
    this.bio = new Person(fName, lName, age, gender);
    this.skills = skills.map(skill => new Skill(skill));
  }
}
```

So much improvement in so few lines! We are now using the constructor to make the code a lot more flexible. With this update, you can use the `Developer` class to create as many types of developer as you need.

Although this solution seems like it will save the day, there is still a tight coupling issue going on in the system. What happens when the constructors in the `Person` and `Skill` classes change? The implication is that you will have to come back and update the call to this constructor in the `Developer` class. Here is an example of such a change in `Skill`:

```
// Skill Class
export class Skill {
  private type: string;
  private yearsOfExperience: number;
  constructor(
    type: string,
    yearsOfExperience: number
  ) {
    this.type = type;
    this.yearsOfExperience = yearsOfExperience
  }
}
```

We added another field to the `yearsOfExperience` class, which is of the number type and represents how long a developer has been practicing a claimed skill. For this to actually work in `Developer`, we have to update the `Developer` class as well:

```
export class Developer {
  public skills: Array<Skill>;
  private bio: Person;
  constructor(
    fName: string,
    lName: string,
    age: number,
    gender: string,
    skils: Array<any>
  ) {
    this.bio = new Person(fName, lName, age, gender);
    this.slills = skills.map(skill =>
        new Skill(skill.type, skill.yearsOfExperience));
  }
}
```

Updating this class every time a dependency changes is what we're are striving to avoid. A common practice is to elevate the constructors of the dependencies to the constructor of the class itself:

```
export class Developer {
  public skills: <Skill>;
  private person: Person;
  constructor(
    skill: Skill,
    person: Person
  ) {}
}
```

This way, the `Developer` is less aware of the implementation details of `Skill` and `Person`. Therefore, if they change internally, `Developer` won't care; it just stays as is.

In fact, TypeScript provides a productivity shorthand:

```
export class Developer {
  constructor(
    public skills: <Skill>,
    private person: Person
  ) {}
}
```

This shorthand will implicitly declare the properties and assign them as dependencies via the constructor as well.

That's not all; elevating these dependencies introduces another challenge. How do we manage all the dependencies in our application without losing track of where things are meant to be? This is where Dependency Injection comes in. It's not an Angular thing, but a popular pattern implemented in Angular.

Let's start seeing DI in action right in an Angular app.

Data in components

To better understand the importance of services and DI, let's create a simple app with a component that shows a list of user comments. Once you have an app created, you can run the following command to generate the required component:

```
ng g component comment-list
```

Update the component's code with the following snippet:

```
import { Component, OnInit } from '@angular/core';

@Component({
  selector: 'app-comment-list',
  templateUrl: './comment-list.component.html',
  styleUrls: ['./comment-list.component.css']
})
export class CommentListComponent implements OnInit {

  comments: Array<any>
  constructor() { }

  ngOnInit() {
    this.comments = [
      {
        author: 'solomon',
```

```
      content: `TypeScript + Angular is amazing`
    },
    {
      author: 'lorna',
      content: `TypeScript is really awesome`
    },
    {
      author: 'codebeast',
      content: `I'm new to TypeScript`
    },
  ];
  }


}
```

The component has a `comments` array, which is populated with hardcoded data once the component is initialized via the `ngOnInit` lifecycle. Now we need to iterate over the list of arrays and print on the DOM:

```html
<div class="list-group">
  <a href="#" class="list-group-item" *ngFor="let comment of comments">
    <h4 class="list-group-item-heading">{{comment.author}}</h4>
    <p class="list-group-item-text">{{comment.content}}</p>
  </a>
</div>
```

You need to include the component in your entry (app) component for it to show up:

```html
<div class="container">
  <h2 class="text-center">TS Comments</h2>
  <div class="col-md-6 col-md-offset-3">
    <app-comment-list></app-comment-list>
  </div>
</div>
```

Your app should look like the following (remember to include Bootstrap as seen in Chapter 2, *Getting Started with TypeScript*):

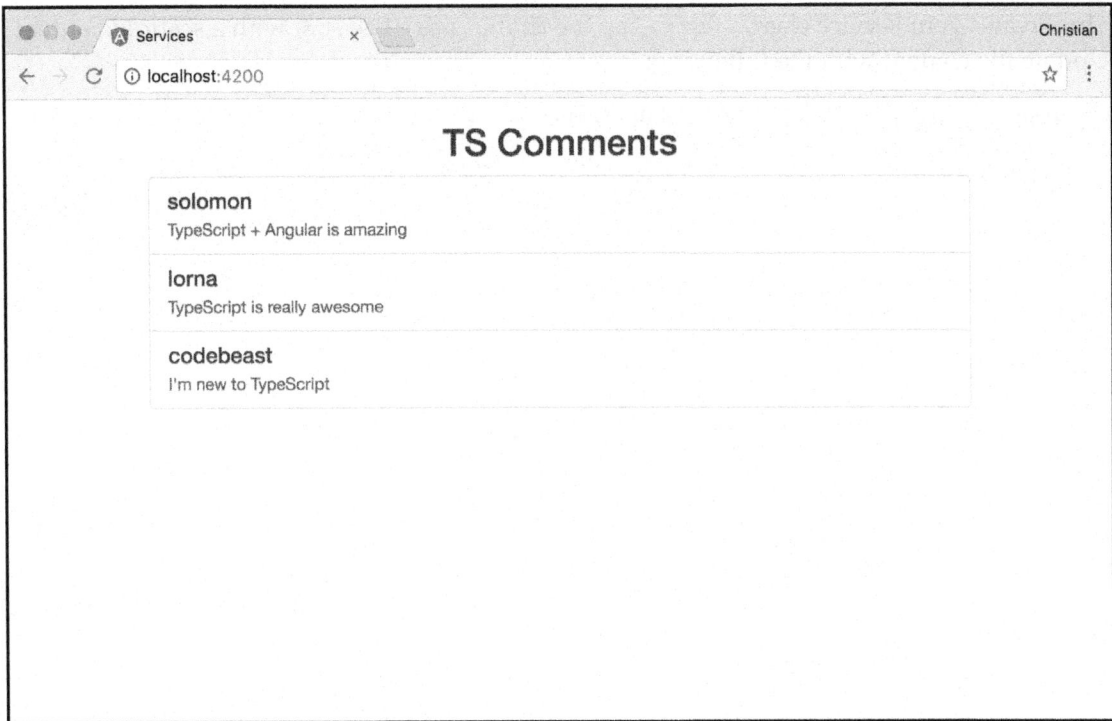

This example works, but the devil lies in the detail. When another component needs a list of comments or a portion of the list, we end up recreating the comments. This is the problem with having data in components.

Data class services

For the sake of reusability and maintainability, we need to abstract the logic concerns out of the component and let the component just serve as a presentation layer. This is one of those use cases where TypeScript services in Angular come into play.

You first need to create a service with the following command:

```
ng g service comment
```

This creates your service class, `./src/app/comment.service.ts`, with a scaffold content. Update the content with the following:

```
import { Injectable } from '@angular/core';

@Injectable()
export class CommentService {
  private comments: Array<any> = [
    {
      author: 'solomon',
      content: `TypeScript + Angular is amazing`
    },
    {
      author: 'lorna',
      content: `TypeScript is really awesome`
    },
    {
      author: 'codebeast',
      content: `I'm new to TypeScript`
    }
  ];
  constructor() {}

  getComments() {
    return this.comments;
  }
}
```

The class now does whatever our component was supposed to do with the data, and the data is fetched using the `getComments` method, which simply returns an array of comments. The `CommentService` class is also decorated; this is not required unless the class has dependencies to be resolved. Nonetheless, good practice demands that we always decorate with `Injectable` to know that a class is meant to be a service.

Back with our list component, we just import the class, resolve the dependency from the constructor to create an instance of the service class, and then populate the property with the `getComments` return value:

```
import { Component, OnInit } from '@angular/core';
import { CommentService } from '../comment.service';

@Component({
  selector: 'app-comment-list',
  templateUrl: './comment-list.component.html',
  styleUrls: ['./comment-list.component.css']
})
export class CommentListComponent implements OnInit {
```

```
private comments: Array<any>;
constructor(
  private commentService: CommentService
) { }

ngOnInit() {
  this.comments = this.commentService.getComments();
}

}
```

Let's attempt to run the app with these current changes in our browser and see whether things still work as expected:

Hell, no! It just blew up. What could have gone wrong? The error message reads **No provider for CommentService!**

Remember that, when we scaffold components with the ng CLI command, the CLI not only creates a component but also adds it to our declaration array in the decorator of ngModule:

```
// ./src/app/app.module.ts
declarations: [
    AppComponent,
    // New scaffolded component here
    CommentListComponent
  ],
```

Modules need to know which components and services belong to them as members. This is why the component is added automatically for you. This is not the same for services because the CLI doesn't automatically update the module (it warns you during the scaffold) when you create service classes via the CLI tool. We need to add the service manually via the providers array:

```
import { CommentService } from './comment.service';
//...

@NgModule({
  //...
  providers: [
    CommentService
  ],
})
export class AppModule { }
```

Now, run the app once more to see how our service now powers the app with no more errors in the console:

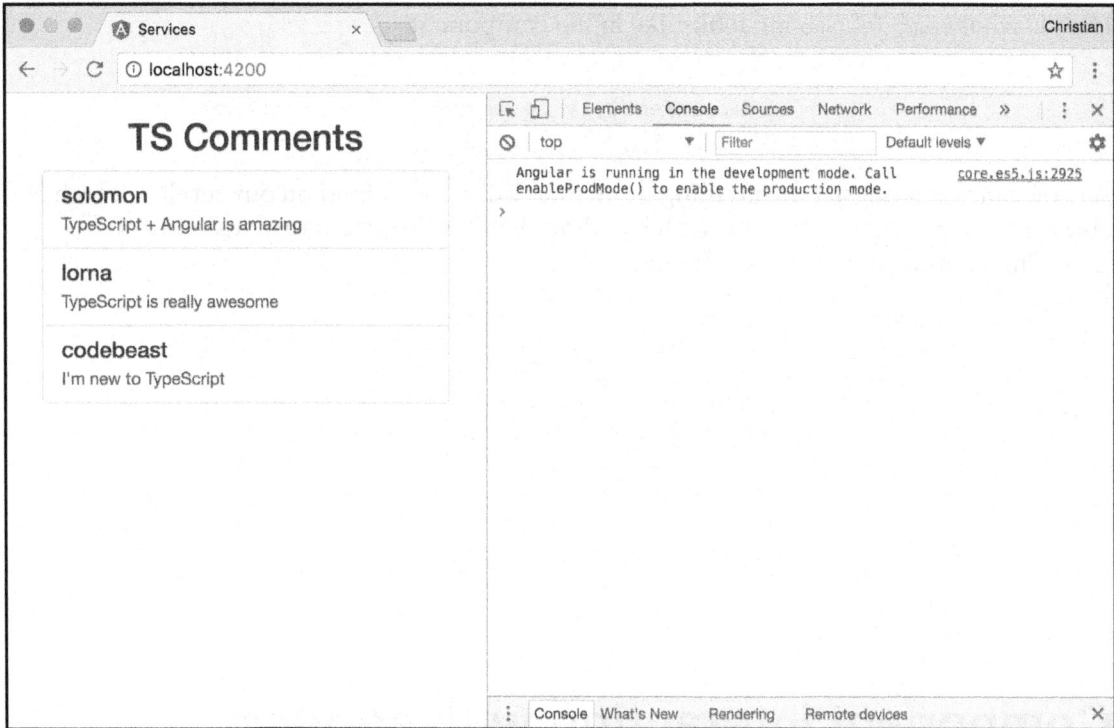

If there is a need to manipulate the data, it must be done in the service and not in the component. Assuming you want to delete a comment by double-clicking on each item in the list, it's fine to receive the event with the component but the actual deletion should be handled by the service.

Start by adding an event listener to the list items:

```
<a href="#" class="list-group-item" (dblclick)="removeComment(comment)"
*ngFor="let comment of comments">
    <h4 class="list-group-item-heading">{{comment.author}}</h4>
    <p class="list-group-item-text">{{comment.content}}</p>
  </a>
```

The dblclick event is triggered by double-clicking the items. When this happens, we call the removeComment method while passing the comment we want to remove from the item.

Here is what `removeComment` looks like in the component:

```
removeComment(comment) {
    this.comments = this.commentService.removeComment(comment);
}
```

As you can see, it doesn't do anything more than calling a method on our service, which is also called `removeComment`. This is the method that has the actual responsibility of removing items from the array of comments:

```
// Comment service
removeComment(removableComment) {
    // find the index of the comment
    const index = this.comments.findIndex(
      comment => comment.author === removableComment.author
    );
    // remove the comment from the array
    this.comments.splice(index, 1);
    // return the new array
    return this.comments;
}
```

Component interaction with services

This is a very handy use case for services. In chapter 6, *Component Composition with TypeScript*, we discussed how components interact with each other and showed different ways of doing it. One of those ways was left out--using a service as an event hub/communication platform for different components.

Let's assume again that, when an item in the list is clicked, we use a sibling component to the comment list component to show a detailed view of the selected comment. First, we need to create this component:

```
ng g component comment-detail
```

Then, you can update the `app.component.html` file to show the added component:

```
<div class="container">
  <h2 class="text-center">TS Comments</h2>
  <div class="col-md-4 col-md-offset-2">
    <app-comment-list></app-comment-list>
  </div>
  <div class="col-md-4">
    <!-- Comment detail component -->
    <app-comment-detail></app-comment-detail>
```

```
    </div>
  </div>
```

Now, we need to define what our component does, because it's empty right now. But before that, let's update the comment service to also serve as a hub between the list component and the sibling detail component:

```
import { Injectable } from '@angular/core';
import { Subject } from 'rxjs/Subject';

@Injectable()
export class CommentService {
  private commentSelectedSource = new Subject<any>();
  public commentSelected$ = this.commentSelectedSource.asObservable();

  private comments: Array<any> = [
   // ...
  ];

  // ...

  showComment(comment) {
    this.commentSelectedSource.next(comment);
  }
}
```

The service now uses an Rx subject to create a stream and a listener, which the selected comment is pushed through and fetched from. The `commentSelectedSource` object is responsible for adding a comment to the stream when the comment is clicked.
The `commetSelected$` object is an observable that we can subscribe to and act on when this comment is clicked.

Now, head right back to your component and add a click event to select the comment item:

```
<div class="list-group">
  <a href="#" class="list-group-item"
    (dblclick)="removeComment(comment)"
    *ngFor="let comment of comments"
    (click)="showComment(comment)"
    >
    <h4 class="list-group-item-heading">{{comment.author}}</h4>
    <p class="list-group-item-text">{{comment.content}}</p>
  </a>
</div>
```

The click event triggers a `showComment` method on the component, which, in turn, calls `showComment` on the service:

```
showComment(comment) {
  this.commentService.showComment(comment);
}
```

We still have to update the comment detail component, so it subscribes to the observable we created in the class:

```
import { Component, OnInit } from '@angular/core';
import { CommentService } from '../comment.service';

@Component({
  selector: 'app-comment-detail',
  templateUrl: './comment-detail.component.html',
  styleUrls: ['./comment-detail.component.css']
})
export class CommentDetailComponent implements OnInit {

  comment: any = {
    author: '',
    content: ''
  };
  constructor(
    private commentService: CommentService
  ) { }

  ngOnInit() {
    this.commentService.commentSelected$.subscribe(comment => {
      this.comment = comment;
    })
  }

}
```

With the `ngOnInit` lifecycle hook, we are able to create a subscription to the observable once the component is ready. There is a comment property that will be bound to the view, and this property is updated via the subscription every time a comment item is clicked. Here is the template for the component showing the selected comment:

```
<div class="panel panel-default" *ngIf="comment.author">
  <div class="panel-heading">{{comment.author}}</div>
  <div class="panel-body">
    {{comment.content}}
  </div>
</div>
```

You can start the app again and try selecting a comment. You should see the following behavior:

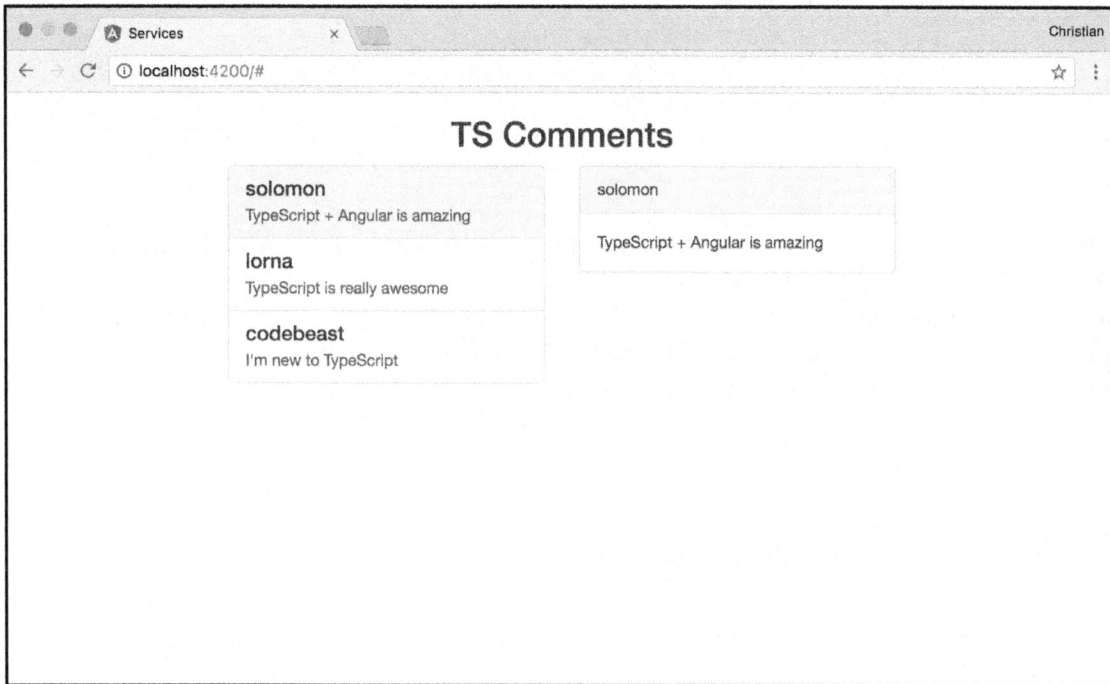

Services as utilities

Apart from managing state and component interaction, services are also known for handling utility operations. Let's say that we want to start collecting new comments in our comment app. We don't know much about forms yet, so we can use the browser's prompt. We expect the user to pass both the username and the content via the same textbox in the prompt, as follows:

```
<username>: <comment content>
```

Therefore, we need a utility method to extract these bits from the textbox into a comment object with the author and content properties. Let's start with collecting the information from the comment list component:

```
showPrompt() {
    const commentString = window.prompt('Please enter your username and
content: ', 'username: content');
    const parsedComment = this.commentService.parseComment(commentString);
    this.commentService.addComment(parsedComment);
}
```

The `showPrompt()` method is used to collect the user input, and the input is passed to the `parseComment` method on the service. This method is an example of a utility method, and we will implement it soon. We will also implement the `addComment` method, which is called with the parsed comment to update the list of comments. Next, add a button to the view with a click event listener that triggers `showPrompt`:

```
<button class="btn btn-primary"
 (click)="showPrompt()"
>Add Comment</button>
```

Add these two methods to the comment service:

```
parseComment(commentString) {
    const commentArr = commentString.split(':');
    const comment = {
      author: commentArr[0].trim(),
      content: commentArr[1].trim()
    }
    return comment;
}

addComment(comment) {
    this.comments.unshift(comment);
}
```

The `parseComment` method takes a string, splits the string, and gets the author and content of the comment. Then, it returns the comment. The addComment method takes a comment and adds it to the list of existing comments.

Now, you can start adding new comments, as shown in the following screenshot:

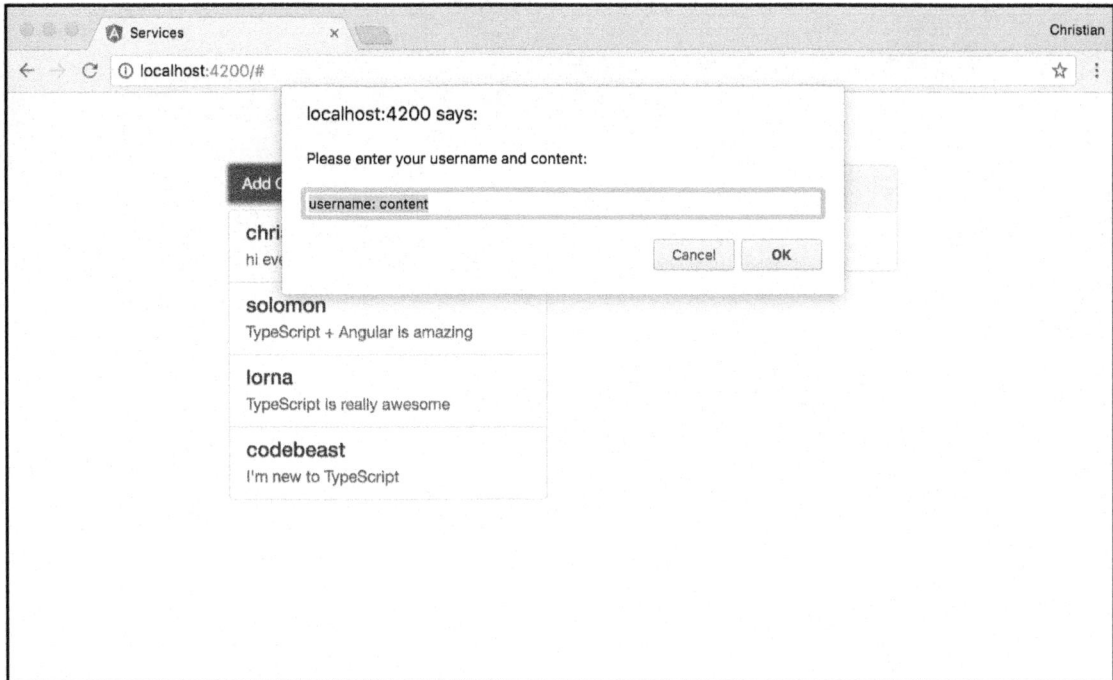

Summary

This chapter exposed a lot of interesting concepts in data abstraction, while utilizing the power of dependency injection. You learned how components interact with each other using a service as a hub, how data and logic are abstracted from a component to services, and how reusable utility code is handled in a service to keep your application clean. In the next chapter, you'll learn a practical approach to forms in Angular and DOM events.

8

Better Forms and Event Handling with TypeScript

Let's talk form. Since the beginning of the book, we have been avoiding form inputs in our examples. This is because I wanted to dedicate this entire chapter to just forms. We will cover as much as it takes to build business applications that collect user information. Here is a breakdown of what you should expect from this chapter:

- Typed form input and output
- Form controls
- Validation
- Form submission and handling
- Event handling
- Control state

Creating types for forms

We want to try to utilize TypeScript as much as possible, as it simplifies our development process and makes our app behavior more predictable. For this reason, we will create a simple data class to serve as a type for the form values.

First, create a new Angular project to follow along with the examples. Then, use the following command to create a new class:

```
ng g class flight
```

The class is generated in the app folder; replace its content with the following data class:

```
export class Flight {
  constructor(
    public fullName: string,
    public from: string,
    public to: string,
    public type: string,
    public adults: number,
    public departure: Date,
    public children?: number,
    public infants?: number,
    public arrival?: Date,
  ) {}
}
```

This class represents all the values our form (yet to be created) will have. The properties that are succeeded by a question mark (?) are optional, which means that TypeScript will throw no errors when the respective values are not supplied.

Before jumping into creating forms, let's start with a clean slate. Replace the app.component.html file with the following:

```
<div class="container">
  <h3 class="text-center">Book a Flight</h3>
  <div class="col-md-offset-3 col-md-6">
    <!-- TODO: Form here -->
  </div>
</div>
```

Run the app and leave it running. You should see the following at port 4200 of localhost (remember to include Bootstrap):

```
●  ●  ●  /  [A] TemplateForms        ×  \                                              Christian
←  →  C   ① localhost:4200                                                          ☆   ○

                               Book a Flight
```

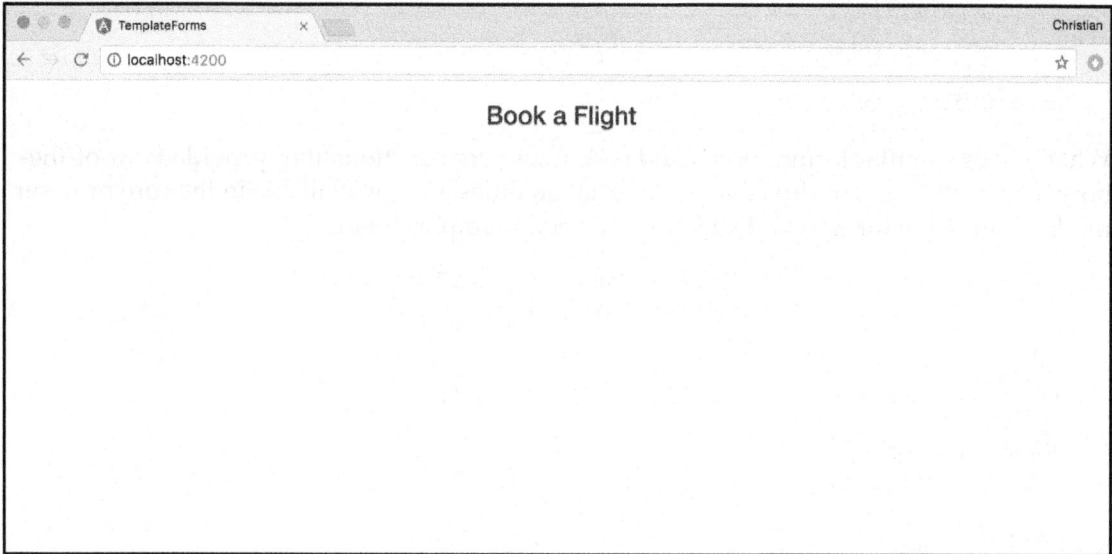

The form module

Now that we have a contract that we want the form to follow, let's now generate the form's component:

```
ng  g component flight-form
```

The command also adds the component as a declaration to our `App` module:

```
import { BrowserModule } from '@angular/platform-browser';
import { NgModule } from '@angular/core';

import { AppComponent } from './app.component';
import { FlightFormComponent } from './flight-form/flight-form.component';

@NgModule({
  declarations: [
    AppComponent,
    // Component added after
    // being generated
    FlightFormComponent
  ],
  imports: [
    BrowserModule
  ],
```

```
    providers: [],
    bootstrap: [AppComponent]
})
export class AppModule { }
```

What makes Angular forms special and easy to use are functionalities provided out-of-the-box, such as the `NgForm` directive. Such functionalities are not available in the core browser module but in the form module. Hence, we need to import them:

```
import { BrowserModule } from '@angular/platform-browser';
import { NgModule } from '@angular/core';

// Import the form module
import { FormsModule } from '@angular/forms';

import { AppComponent } from './app.component';
import { FlightFormComponent } from './flight-form/flight-form.component';

@NgModule({
  declarations: [
    AppComponent,
    FlightFormComponent
  ],
  imports: [
    BrowserModule,
    // Add the form module
    // to imports array
    FormsModule
  ],
  providers: [],
  bootstrap: [AppComponent]
})
export class AppModule { }
```

Simply importing and adding `FormModule` to the `imports` array is all we needed to do.

Two-way binding

The perfect time to start showing some form controls using the form component in the browser is right now. Keeping the state in sync between the data layer (model) and the view can be very challenging, but with Angular it's just a matter of using one directive exposed from `FormModule`:

```
<!-- ./app/flight-form/flight-form.component.html -->
<form>
```

```
    <div class="form-group">
      <label for="fullName">Full Name</label>
      <input
        type="text"
        class="form-control"
        [(ngModel)]="flightModel.fullName"
        name="fullName"
      >
    </div>
  </form>
```

Angular relies on the `name` attribute internally to carry out binding. For this reason, the `name` attribute is required.

Pay attention to `[(ngModel)]="flightModel.fullName"`; it's trying to bind a property on the component class to the form. This model will be of the `Flight` type, which is the class we created earlier:

```
// ./app/flight-form/flight-form.component.ts

import { Component, OnInit } from '@angular/core';
import { Flight } from '../flight';

@Component({
  selector: 'app-flight-form',
  templateUrl: './flight-form.component.html',
  styleUrls: ['./flight-form.component.css']
})
export class FlightFormComponent implements OnInit {
  flightModel: Flight;
  constructor() {
    this.flightModel = new Flight('', '', '', '', 0, '', 0, 0, '');
  }

  ngOnInit() {}
}
```

The `flightModel` property is added to the component as a `Flight` type and initialized with some default values.

Include the component in the app HTML, so it can be displayed in the browser:

```
<div class="container">
  <h3 class="text-center">Book a Flight</h3>
  <div class="col-md-offset-3 col-md-6">
```

```
      <app-flight-form></app-flight-form>
    </div>
  </div>
```

This is what you should have in the browser:

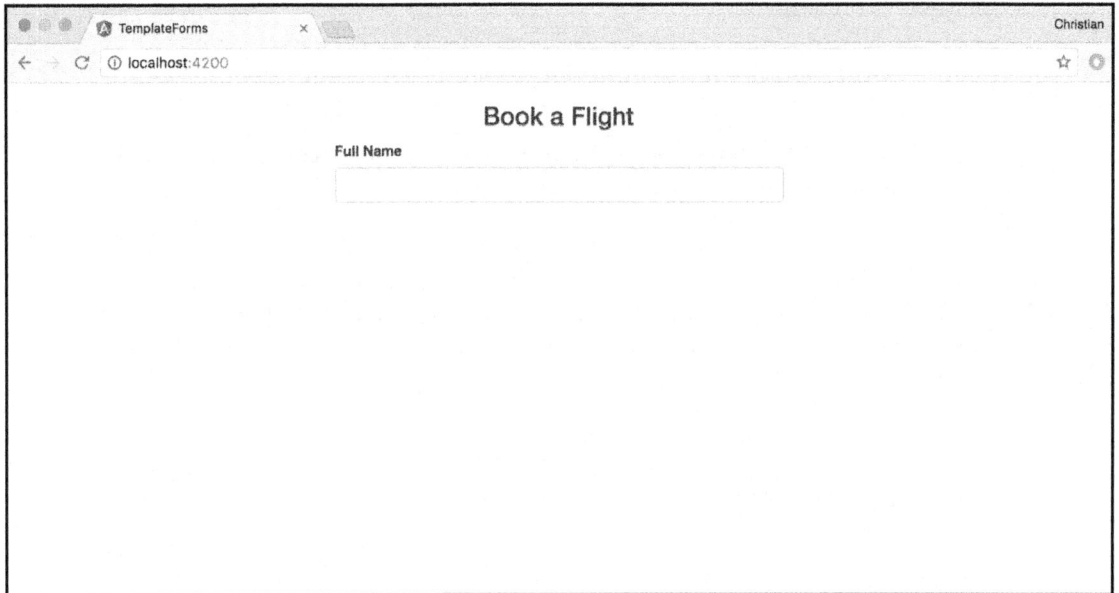

To see two-way binding in action, use interpolation to display the value of
flightModel.fullName. Then, enter a value and see the live update:

```
<form>
  <div class="form-group">
    <label for="fullName">Full Name</label>
    <input
      type="text"
      class="form-control"
      [(ngModel)]="flightModel.fullName"
      name="fullName"
    >
    {{flightModel.fullName}}
  </div>
</form>
```

Here is what it looks like:

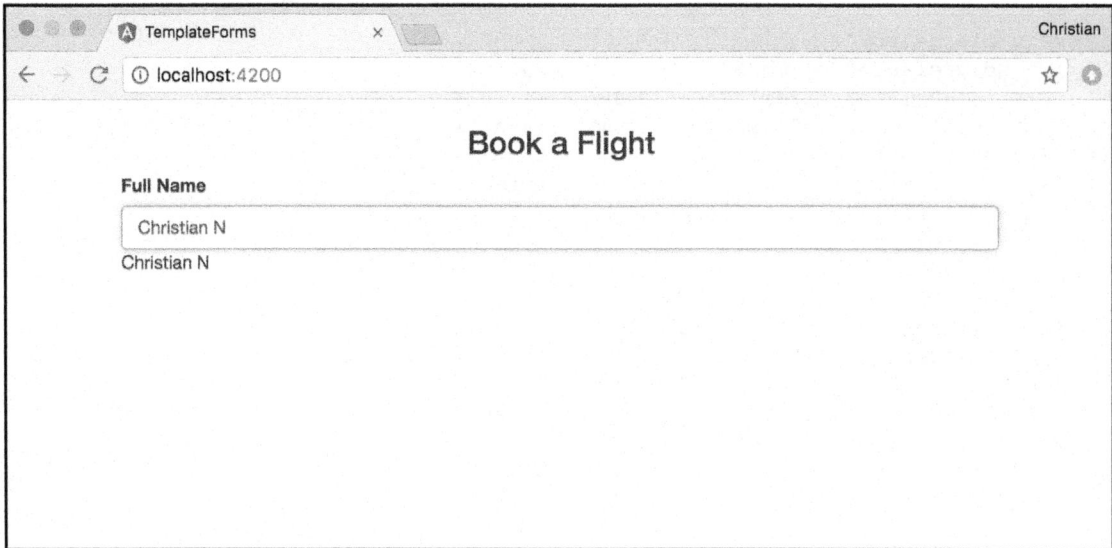

More form fields

Let's get hands-on and add the remaining form fields. After all, we can't book a flight by just supplying our names.

The `from` and `to` fields are going to be *select boxes* with a list of cities we can fly into and out of. This list of cities will be stored right in our component class, and then we can iterate over it in the template and render it as a select box:

```
export class FlightFormComponent implements OnInit {
  flightModel: Flight;
  // Array of cities
  cities:Array<string> = [
    'Lagos',
    'Mumbai',
    'New York',
    'London',
    'Nairobi'
  ];
  constructor() {
    this.flightModel = new Flight('', '', '', '', 0, '', 0, 0, '');
  }
}
```

The array stores a few cities from around the world as strings. Let's now use the `ngFor` directive to iterate over the cities and display them on the form using a select box:

```
<div class="row">
    <div class="col-md-6">
        <label for="from">From</label>
        <select type="text" id="from" class="form-control"
[(ngModel)]="flightModel.from" name="from">
            <option *ngFor="let city of cities"
value="{{city}}">{{city}}</option>
        </select>
    </div>
    <div class="col-md-6">
        <label for="to">To</label>
        <select type="text" id="to" class="form-control"
[(ngModel)]="flightModel.to" name="to">
            <option *ngFor="let city of cities"
value="{{city}}">{{city}}</option>
        </select>
    </div>
</div>
```

Neat and clean! You can open the browser and see it right there:

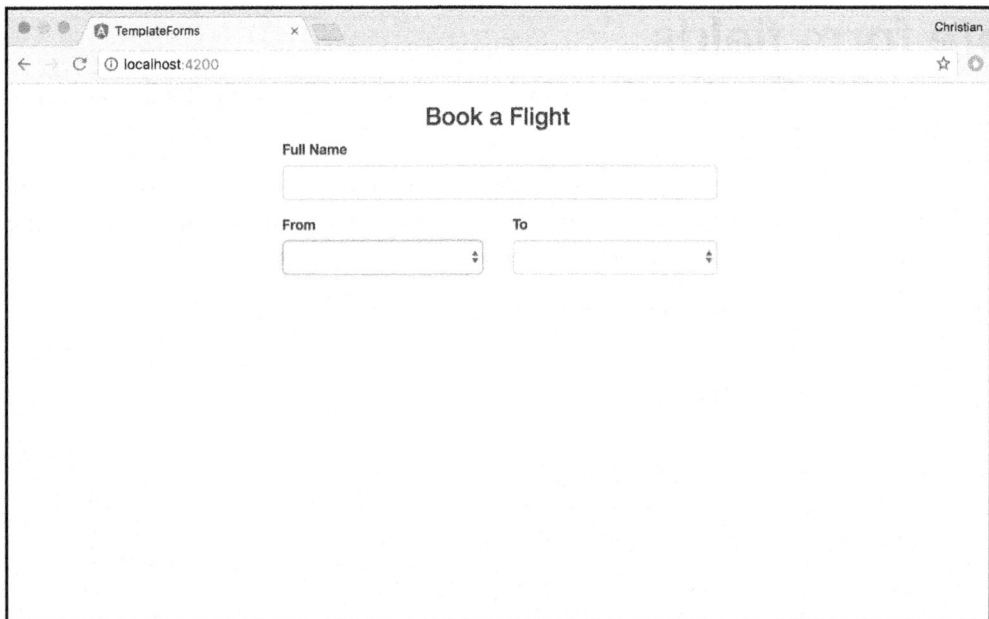

The select drop-down, when clicked, shows a list of cities, as expected:

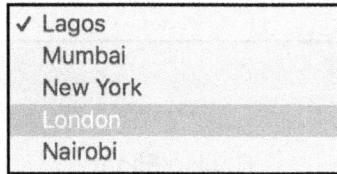

```
✓ Lagos
  Mumbai
  New York
  London
  Nairobi
```

Next, let's add the trip type field (radio buttons), the departure date field (date control), and the arrival date field (date control):

```html
<div class="row" style="margin-top: 15px">
    <div class="col-md-5">
      <label for="" style="display: block">Trip Type</label>
      <label class="radio-inline">
        <input type="radio" name="type" [(ngModel)]="flightModel.type"
value="One Way"> One way
      </label>
      <label class="radio-inline">
        <input type="radio" name="type" [(ngModel)]="flightModel.type"
value="Return"> Return
      </label>
    </div>
    <div class="col-md-4">
      <label for="departure">Departure</label>
      <input type="date" id="departure" class="form-control"
[(ngModel)]="flightModel.departure" name="departure">
    </div>
    <div class="col-md-3">
      <label for="arrival">Arrival</label>
      <input type="date" id="arrival" class="form-control"
[(ngModel)]="flightModel.arrival" name="arrival">
    </div>
  </div>
```

How the data is bound to the controls is very similar to the text and select fields that we created previously. The major difference is the types of control (radio buttons and dates):

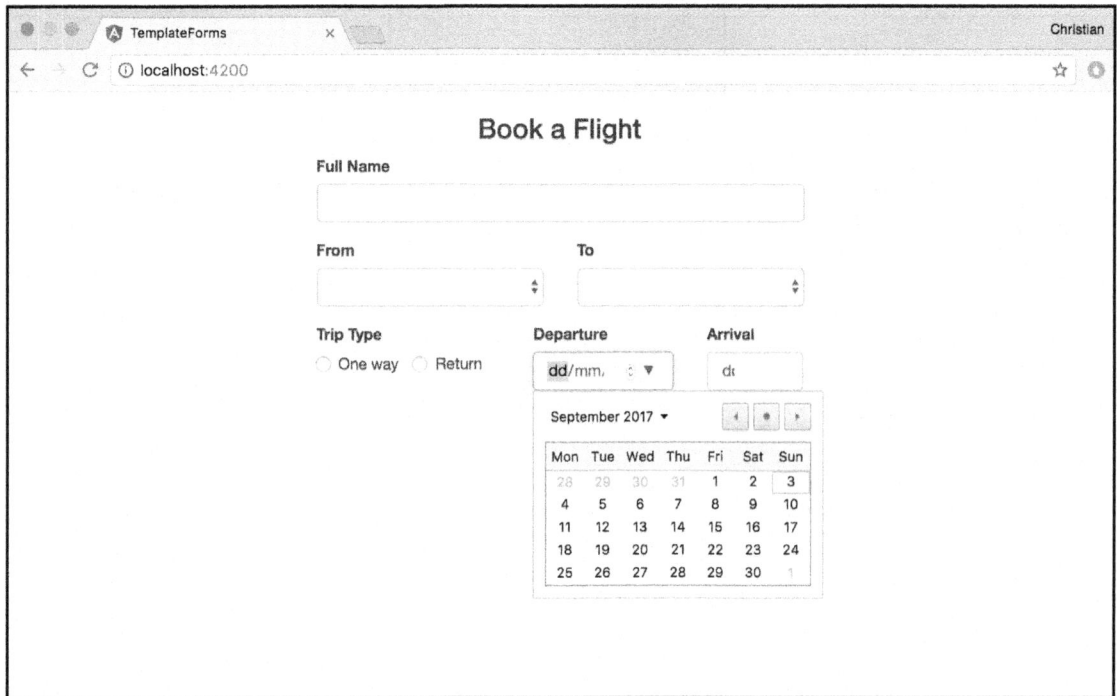

Lastly, add the number of passengers (adults, children, and infants):

```
<div class="row" style="margin-top: 15px">
    <div class="col-md-4">
      <label for="adults">Adults</label>
      <input type="number" id="adults" class="form-control"
[(ngModel)]="flightModel.adults" name="adults">
    </div>
    <div class="col-md-4">
      <label for="children">Children</label>
      <input type="number" id="children" class="form-control"
[(ngModel)]="flightModel.children" name="children">
    </div>
    <div class="col-md-4">
      <label for="infants">Infants</label>
      <input type="number" id="infants" class="form-control"
[(ngModel)]="flightModel.infants" name="infants">
    </div>
  </div>
```

The passengers section are all of the number type because we are just expected to pick the number of passengers coming onboard from each category:

Validating the form and form fields

Angular greatly simplifies form validation by using its built-in directives and state properties. You can use the state property to check whether a form field has been touched. If it's touched but violates a validation rule, you can use the `ngIf` directive to display associated errors.

Let's see an example of validating the full name field:

```
<div class="form-group">
    <label for="fullName">Full Name</label>
    <input
      type="text"
      id="fullName"
      class="form-control"
      [(ngModel)]="flightModel.fullName"
      name="fullName"

      #name="ngModel"
```

```
        required
        minlength="6">
  </div>
```

We just added three extra significant attributes to our form's full name field: #name, required, and minlength. The #name attribute is completely different from the name attribute in that the former is a template variable that holds information about this given field via the ngModel value while the latter is the usual form input name attribute.

In Angular, validation rules are passed as attributes, which is why required and minlength are there.

Yes, the fields are validated, but there are no feedbacks to the user on what must have gone wrong. Let's add some error messages to be shown when form fields are violated:

```
<div *ngIf="name.invalid && (name.dirty || name.touched)" class="text-
danger">
    <div *ngIf="name.errors.required">
      Name is required.
    </div>
    <div *ngIf="name.errors.minlength">
      Name must be at least 6 characters long.
    </div>
  </div>
```

The ngIf directive shows these div elements conditionally:

- If the form field has been touched but there's no value in it, the **Name is required** error is shown
- **Name must be at least 6 characters long** is also shown when the field is touched but the content length is less than 6.

The following two screenshots show these error outputs in the browser:

A different error is shown when a value is entered but the value text count is not up to 6:

Submitting forms

We need to consider a few factors before submitting a form:

- Is the form valid?
- Is there a handler for the form prior to submission?

To make sure that the form is valid, we can disable the **Submit** button:

```
<form #flightForm="ngForm">
  <div class="form-group" style="margin-top: 15px">
    <button class="btn btn-primary btn-block"
[disabled]="!flightForm.form.valid">
      Submit
    </button>
  </div>
</form>
```

First, we add a template variable called `flightForm` to the form and then use the variable to check whether the form is valid. If the form is invalid, we disable the button from being clicked:

To handle the submission, add an `ngSubmit` event to the form. This event will be called when the button is clicked:

```
<form #flightForm="ngForm" (ngSubmit)="handleSubmit()">
  ...
</form>
```

You can now add a class method, `handleSubmit`, to handle the form submission. A simple log to the console may be just enough for this example:

```
export class FlightFormComponent implements OnInit {
  flightModel: Flight;
  cities:Array<string> = [
    ...
  ];
  constructor() {
    this.flightModel = new Flight('', '', '', '', 0, '', 0, 0, '');
  }

  // Handle for submission
  handleSubmit() {
    console.log(this.flightModel);
  }
}
```

Handling events

Forms are not the only way we receive values from users. Simple DOM interactions, mouse clicks, and keyboard interactions can raise events that could lead to a request from our users. Of course, we have to handle their requests one way or another. There are numerous events that we can't talk about in this book. What we can do is look at basic keyboard and mouse events.

Mouse events

To demonstrate the two popular mouse events, click and double-click, create a new Angular project and then add the following autogenerated `app.component.html`:

```html
<div class="container">
  <div class="row">
    <h3 class="text-center">
      {{counter}}
    </h3>
    <div class="buttons">
      <div class="btn btn-primary">
        Increment
      </div>
      <div class="btn btn-danger">
        Decrement
      </div>
    </div>
  </div>
</div>
```

A `counter` property is bound to the view using interpolation and **Increment** and **Decrement** buttons. The property is available on the app component and is initialized to zero:

```typescript
import { Component } from '@angular/core';

@Component({
  selector: 'app-root',
  templateUrl: './app.component.html',
  styleUrls: ['./app.component.css']
})
export class AppComponent {
  counter = 0;
}
```

The following is what it baically looks like:

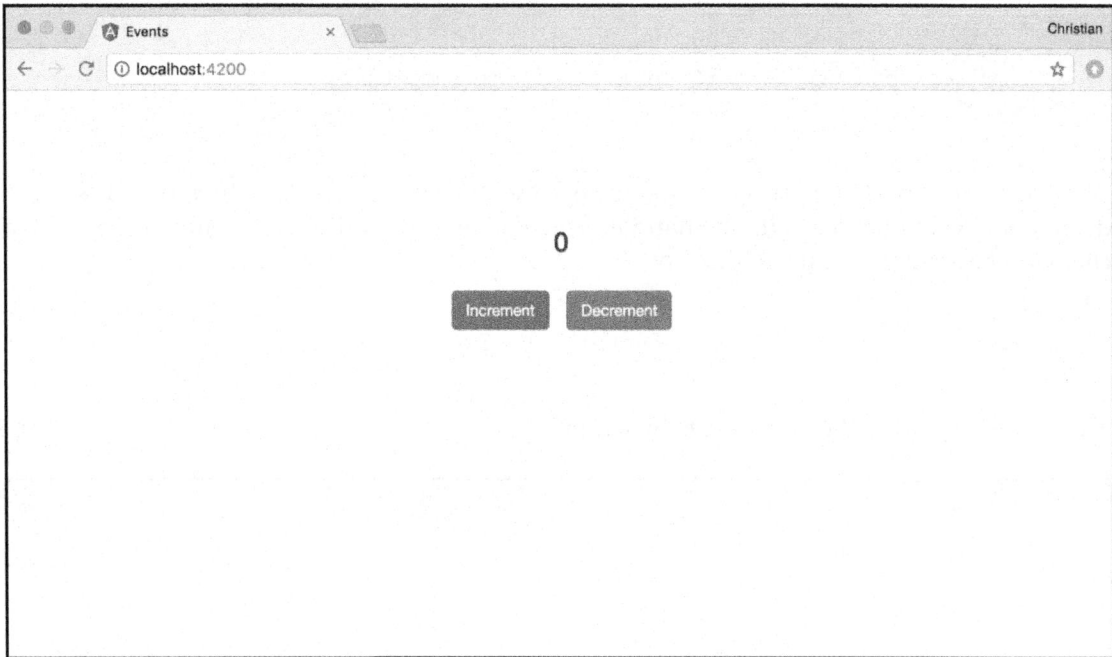

Clicking the buttons does absolutely nothing. Let's add a click event to the **Increment** button, so it adds 1 to the counter property every time it's clicked:

```
export class AppComponent {
  counter = 0;
  increment() {
    this.counter++
  }
}
```

We need to bind this event handler to the button in the template for us to actually increment the counter when the button is clicked:

```
<div class="btn btn-primary" (click)="increment()">
    Increment
</div>
```

Events are bound to the template using attributes but wrapping the attribute in parentheses. The attribute value becomes the method on the component class that will serve as the event handler.

We need the same functionality for Decrement. Assuming that decrementing is an action you want to ensure that the user intended to implement, you can attach a double-click event:

```
<div class="btn btn-danger" (dblclick)="decrement()">
  Decrement
</div>
```

As you can see, instead of using `click`, we use the `dblclick` event and then bind the decrement event handler to it. The handler is just an inverse of the increment handler with a check to see whether we have hit zero:

```
decrement() {
   this.counter <= 0 ? (this.counter = 0) : this.counter--;
}
```

The following shows the new events in action:

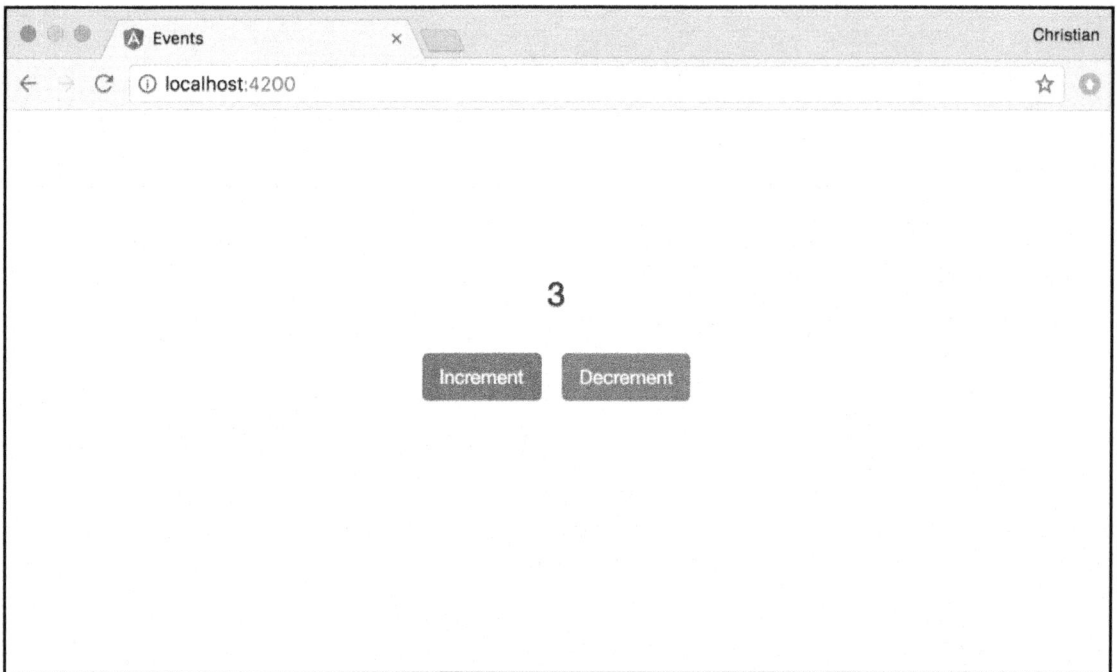

Keyboard events

You can track keyboard interactions by listening to various keyboard events. The `keypress` event tells you that a button is clicked; if you have a listener attached to it, the listener is fired. You can attach keyboard events in the same way that we attached mouse events:

```
<div class="container" (keypress)="showKey($event)" tabindex="1">
  ...
  <div class="key-bg" *ngIf="keyPressed">
    <h1>{{key}}</h1>
  </div>
<div>
```

The element with the `key-bg` class is shown when a key is pressed; it displays the exact key we pressed, which is held in the `key` property. The `keyPressed` property is a Boolean that we set to `true` when a key is pressed.

The event fires the `showKey` listener; let's implement it:

```
import { Component } from '@angular/core';

@Component({
  selector: 'app-root',
  templateUrl: './app.component.html',
  styleUrls: ['./app.component.css']
})
export class AppComponent {
  keyPressed = false;
  key = '';
  // ....
  showKey($event) {
    this.keyPressed = true;
    this.key = $event.key.toUpperCase();
    setTimeout(() => {
      this.keyPressed = false;
    }, 500)
  }
}
```

The `showKey` handler does the following:

- It sets the `key` property with the value of the pressed key
- The pressed key is represented as a lowercase string, so we use the `toUpperCase` method to transform it to uppercase
- The `keyPressed` property is set to `true`, so it displays the pressed key, and is then set to `false` after 500 miliseconds, so the shown key is hidden

When you press a key (and the `container` div has focus), the following screenshot shows what happens:

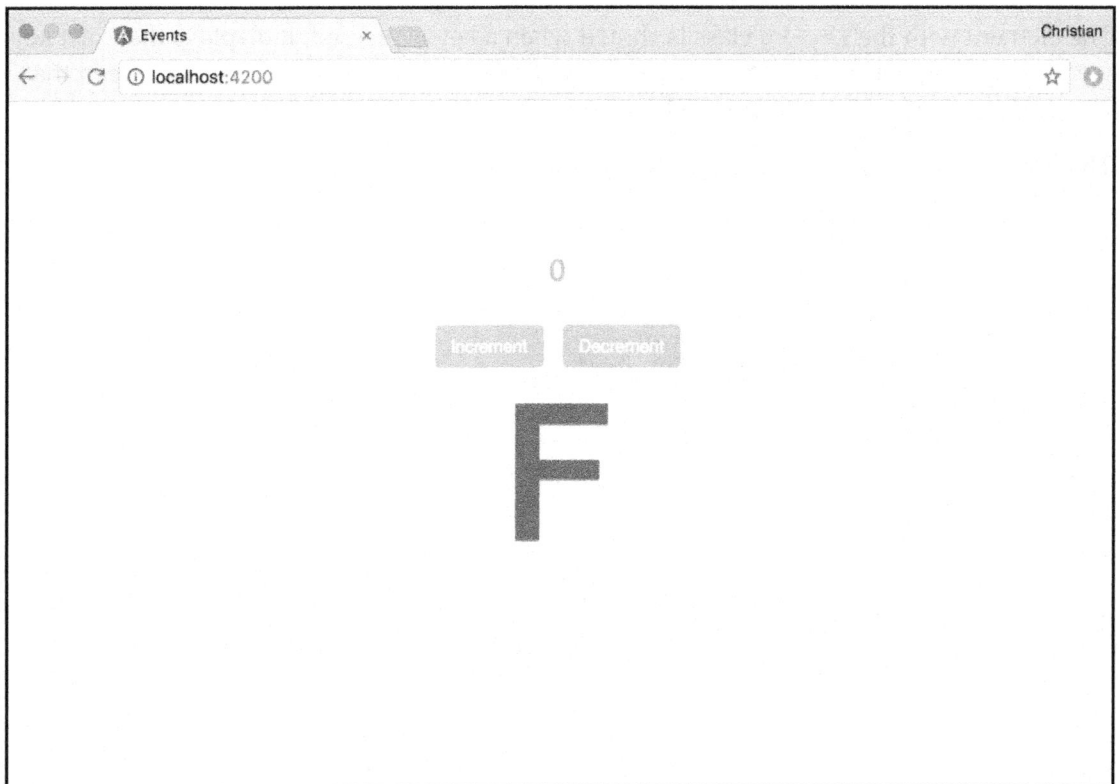

Summary

You now have a great deal of knowledge about collecting user inputs either via forms or events. We also covered important features of forms, such as typed inputs, validation, two-way binding, submission, and so on. The event examples we saw covered both mouse and keyboard events and how to handle them. All these interesting encounters prepare you for building business applications.

9

Writing Modules, Directives, and Pipes with TypeScript

Modularity is essential for building large software systems, and Angular projects are not an exception to this. When our app starts growing, managing its different members in one entry module starts becoming really difficult and confusing. It becomes more challenging when you have a lot of services, directives, and pipes. Speaking of directives and pipes, we will take some time to discuss their use cases and examples in this chapter, while taking a journey in managing our application better with modules.

Directives

DOM manipulation is not always best handled in components. Components should be as lean as possible; this way, things are kept simple and your code can easily be moved around and reused. So, where should we handle DOM manipulation then? The answer is directives. Just like you should take data manipulation tasks to services, best practices suggest you take heavy DOM manipulations to directives.

There are three types of directives in Angular:

- Components
- Attribute directives
- Structural directives

Yes, components! Components are qualified directives. They are directives with a direct access to the template being manipulated. We have already seen components enough in this book; let's focus on the attribute and structural directives.

Attribute directives

This category of directives is known for adding behavioral features to the DOM but not removing or adding any DOM content. Things such as changing appearance, showing or hiding elements, manipulating elements' attributes, and so on.

To better understand attribute directives, let's build some UI directives that are applied to component templates. These directives will change the behavior of the DOM when they are applied.

Create a new directive in a fresh project with the following command:

```
ng generate directive ui-button
```

This will create an empty directive in the app folder with the following content:

```
import { Directive } from '@angular/core';

@Directive({
  selector: '[appUiButton]'
})
export class UiButtonDirective {
  constructor() {}
}
```

The `Directive` decorator is first imported from the `@angular/core` module. The decorator is used on any class that is expected to act as a directive. Just like decorators on components, the directive decorator takes an object with a selector property. When this selector is applied to the DOM, the behavior of the directive is exhibited.

The behavior we are trying to achieve in this example entails styling a completely unstyled button with just a single attribute. Let's assume that we have the following button in our app component:

```
<div class="container">
  <button>Click!!</button>
</div>
```

This is just a simple boring button on the screen:

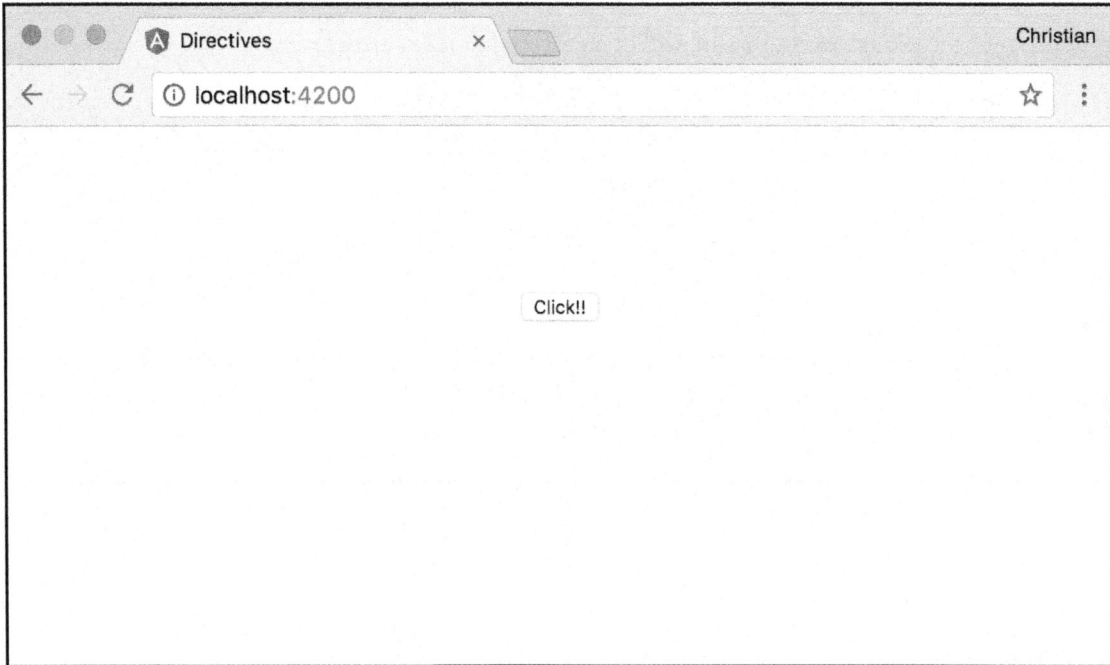

To use the attribute directive we just created, add it as a *value-less* attribute to the button:

```
<button appUiButton>Click!!</button>
```

Next, find a way to access the button element from the `directive` class. We need this access to be able to apply styles to the button, right from the class. Thanks to the `ElementRef` class, which, when injected to the directive via the constructor, gives us access to the native element, which is where the button element can be accessed:

```
import { Directive, ElementRef } from '@angular/core';

@Directive({
  selector: '[appUiButton]'
})
export class UiButtonDirective {
  constructor(el: ElementRef) {
  }
}
```

It is injected and resolved into the `el` property. We can access the button element from the property:

```
import { Directive, ElementRef } from '@angular/core';

@Directive({
  selector: '[appUiButton]'
})
export class UiButtonDirective {
  constructor(el: ElementRef) {
    el.nativeElement.style.backgroundColor = '#ff00a6';
  }
}
```

The `nativeElement` property gives you access to the element that the attribute directive was applied to. You can then treat the value like a DOM API, which is why we can access the `style` and `backgroundColor` properties:

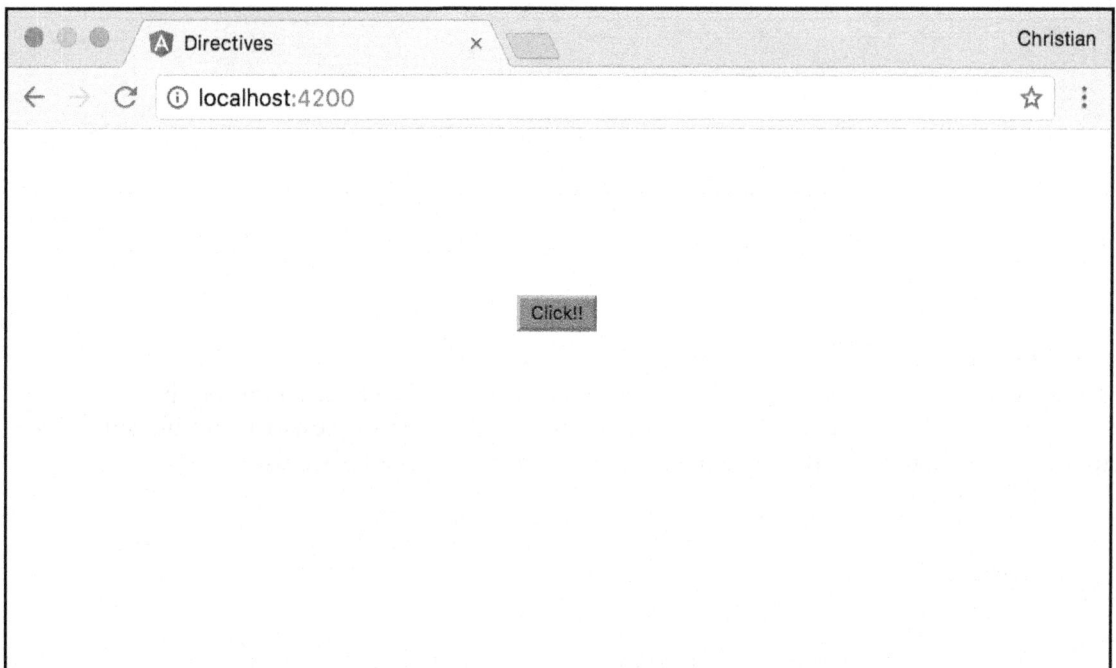

You can see that the pink background was applied effectively. Let's make the button more interesting with more styles, right from the directive:

```
import { Directive, ElementRef } from '@angular/core';

@Directive({
  selector: '[appUiButton]'
})
export class UiButtonDirective {
  constructor(el: ElementRef) {
    Object.assign(el.nativeElement.style, {
      backgroundColor: '#ff00a6',
      padding: '7px 15px',
      fontSize: '16px',
      color: '#fff',
      border: 'none',
      borderRadius: '4px'
    })
  }
}
```

Instead of setting the values using several dots, we just use the `Object.assign` method to reduce the amount of code we have to write. Now, we have a prettier button in the browser, completely styled with a directive:

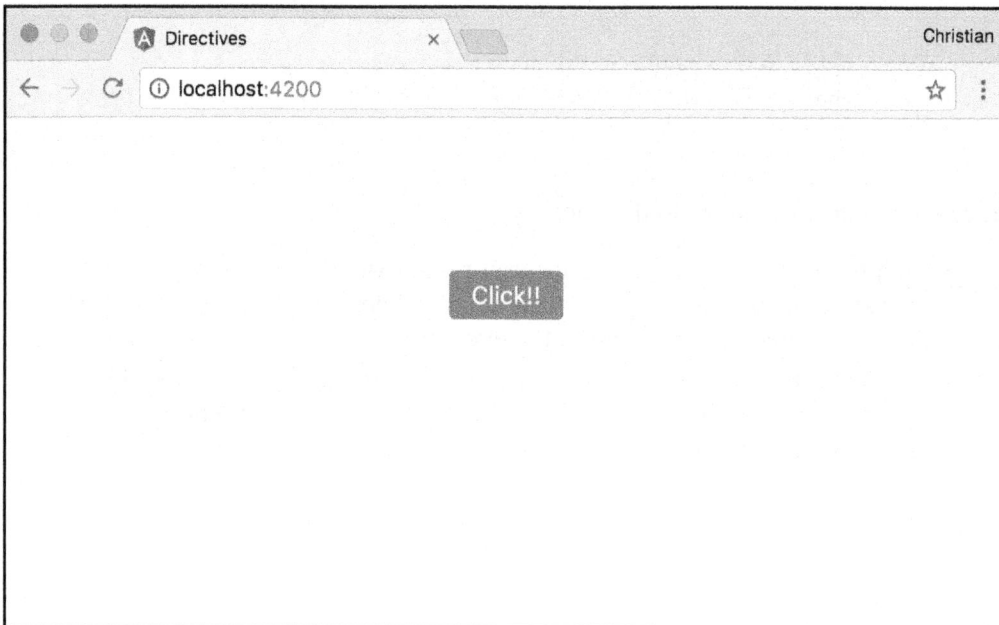

Handling events in directives

Directives are so flexible that they allow you to apply different states, based on events triggered by the user. For instance, we can add a hover behavior to the button where a different color (say black) is applied to the button when the mouse cursor moves over the button:

```typescript
import {
  Directive,
  ElementRef,
  HostListener } from '@angular/core';

@Directive({
  selector: '[appUiButton]'
})
export class UiButtonDirective {
  constructor(private el: ElementRef) {
    Object.assign(el.nativeElement.style, {
      backgroundColor: '#ff00a6',
      ...
    })
  }

  @HostListener('mouseenter') onMouseEnter() {
    this.el.nativeElement.style.backgroundColor = '#000';
  }

  @HostListener('mouseleave') onMouseLeave() {
    this.el.nativeElement.style.backgroundColor = '#ff00a6';
  }
}
```

We introduced a few members to this file:

- We import HostListener, a decorator that extends a method in the class. It turns the method into an event listener attached to the native element. The decorator takes an argument of the event type.
- We define two methods on onMouseEnter and onMouseLeave and then decorate the methods with HostListener. These methods change the background colors of the button when a hover occurs.

Here is what the behavior looks like when we hover the mouse over the button:

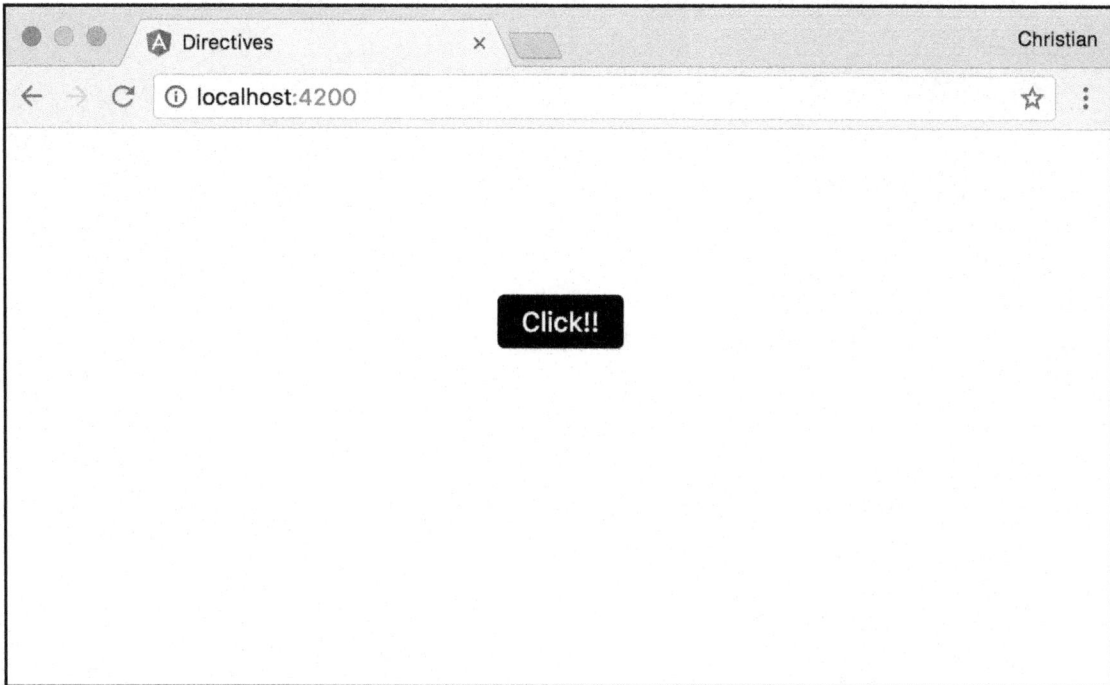

Dynamic attribute directives

What if we, the authors of this directive, are the final consumers? What if another developer is reusing the directive as an API? How do we make it flexible enough with dynamic values? When you ask yourself these questions while writing directives, then it's time to make it dynamic.

All this while, we have been using the directive without any value. We can actually use attribute values to receive inputs into the directive:

```
<button appUiButton bgColor="red">Click!!</button>
```

We added a new attribute, bgColor, which is not a directive but an input property. The property is used to send dynamic values to the directive, as follows:

```typescript
import {
  Directive,
  ElementRef,
  HostListener,
  Input,
  OnInit } from '@angular/core';

@Directive({
  selector: '[appUiButton]'
})
export class UiButtonDirective implements OnInit {
  @Input() bgColor: string;
  @Input() hoverBgColor: string;
  constructor(private el: ElementRef) {}

  ngOnInit() {
    Object.assign(this.el.nativeElement.style, {
      backgroundColor: this.bgColor || '#ff00a6',
      padding: '7px 15px',
      fontSize: '16px',
      color: '#fff',
      border: 'none',
      borderRadius: '4px'
    })
  }

  @HostListener('mouseenter') onMouseEnter() {
    console.log(this.bgColor);
    this.el.nativeElement.style.backgroundColor = this.hoverBgColor ||
'#000';
  }

  @HostListener('mouseleave') onMouseLeave() {
    this.el.nativeElement.style.backgroundColor = this.bgColor ||
'#ff00a6';
  }
}
```

Here are the changes we introduced:

- Two `Input` decorated properties--`bgColor` and `bgHoverColor`--are introduced to serve as the flow of dynamic values from the template to the directive.
- The setup of this directive is moved from the constructor to the `ngOnInit` method. This is because the input decorator is set by Angular's change detection, which doesn't happen in a constructor, thereby making `bgColor` and `bgHoverColor` undefined when we try to access them from the constructor.
- When setting up the styles, rather than hardcoding the value of `backgroundColor`, we use the value received via `bgColor`. We also have a fallback value just in case the developer forgets to include the attribute.
- The same thing happens to the mouse-enter and mouse-leave events.

Now, the button visuals are affected by dynamic values:

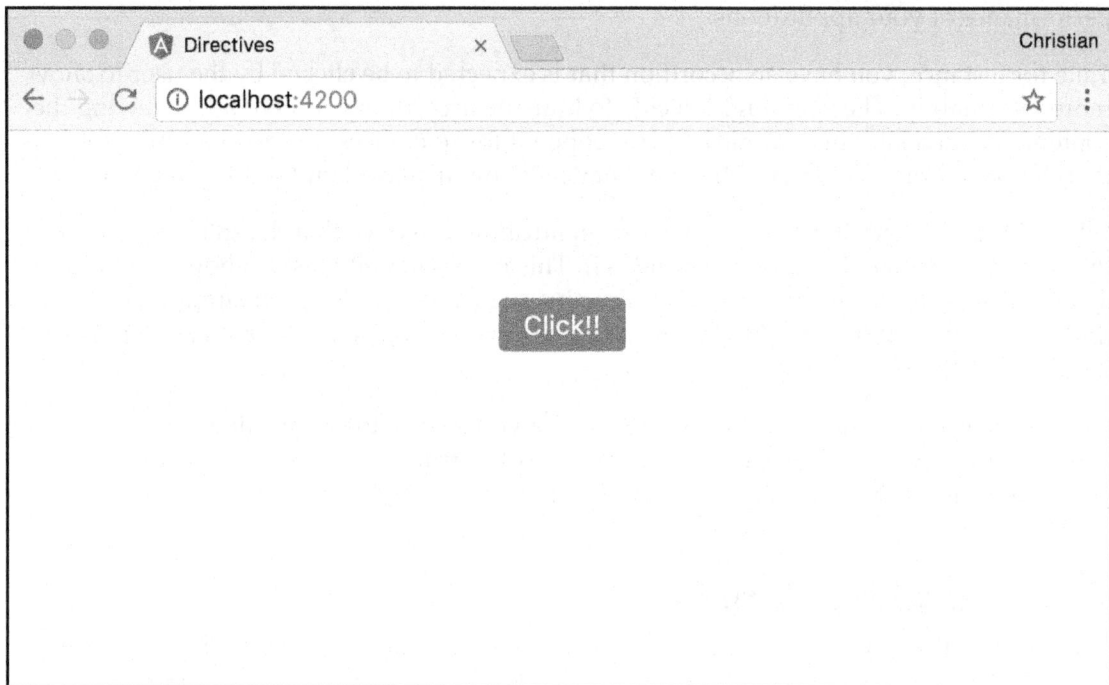

Structural directives

Structural directives have a lot in common with attribute directives, in terms of how they are created, but they are very different in how they are expected to behave. A structural directive, unlike an attribute directive, is expected to create or remove a DOM element. This is different from using a CSS display property to show or hide an element. In this case, the element is still in the DOM tree but is not visible to the end user when hidden.

A good example is `*ngIf`. When an element is removed from the DOM using an `*ngIf` structural directive, the directive both disappears from the screen and gets deleted from the DOM tree.

Why the difference?

The way you control the visibility of DOM elements could have a great impact on the performance of your applications.

Take for instance, you have an accordion that is expected to be clicked by the user to show more information. The user might decide to hide the accordion's content after viewing the content and, at a later time, come back to reopen it for references. It starts becoming obvious that the accordion's content has the tendency of being displayed and hidden at any time.

When this is the case, it is best that we use an attribute directive that doesn't hide/remove the accordion content but rather just hides it. This makes it really fast to show and hide again when needed. Using a structural directive such as `*ngIf` keeps creating and destroying a part of the DOM tree, which can be very expensive if the DOM content being controlled is huge.

On the other hand, when you have some content you're sure the user will view only once or a maximum of two times, it is better to make use of a structural directive such as `*ngIf`. This way, your DOM is not littered with lots of unused HTML contents.

The deal with asterisks

The asterisks that precede all the structural directives are very important. The `*ngIf` and `*ngFor` directives refuse to work when you remove the asterisks from them, implying that the asterisks are required. The question, therefore, is this: why do the asterisks have to be there?

They are syntactic sugar in Angular, meaning that they don't have to be written this way. This is how they actually look:

```
<div template="ngIf true">
  <p>Lorem ipsum dolor sit amet, consectetur adipisicing elit. Nesciunt non
perspiciatis consequatur sapiente provident nemo similique. Minus quo
veritatis ratione, quaerat dolores optio facilis dolor nemo, tenetur,
obcaecati quibusdam, doloremque.</p>
</div>
```

This template attribute is, in turn, translated into the following by Angular:

```
<ng-template [ngIf]="true">
  <div template="ngIf true">
    <p>Lorem ipsum dolor sit amet, consectetur adipisicing elit....</p>
  </div>
</ng-template>
```

See how `ngIf` has now become a normal Angular property but is injected into a template. When the value is `false`, the template is removed (not hidden) from the DOM tree. Writing such directives this way is just a lot of code to write, so Angular added the syntactic sugar to simplify how we write the `ngIf` directive:

```
<div *ngIf="true">
  <p>Lorem ipsum dolor sit amet, consectetur adipisicing elit. Nesciunt non
perspiciatis consequatur sapiente provident nemo similique.</p>
</div>
```

Creating structural directives

We have already seen how to use structural directives from our previous examples. How do we create them? We create them in the same way we created the attribute directive, by running the following command in your terminal:

```
ng generate directive when
```

Yes, we are naming the directive `when`. This directive does exactly what `*ngIf` does, so, hopefully, it will help you better understand the internals of the directive you've already used.

Update the directive with the following:

```
import {
  Directive,
  Input,
  TemplateRef,
  ViewContainerRef } from '@angular/core';

@Directive({
  selector: '[appWhen]'
})
export class WhenDirective {
  constructor(
    private templateRef: TemplateRef<any>,
    private viewContainer: ViewContainerRef) { }
}
```

We introduced a few members you're not familiar with yet. `TemplateRef` is a reference to the `ng-template` template that we saw earlier, in which the DOM content we are controlling is contained. `ViewContainerRef` is a reference to the view itself.

When using the `appWhen` directive in the view, it's expected to take a condition such as `ngIf`. To receive such a condition, we need to create a decorated `Input` setter method:

```
export class WhenDirective {
  private hasView = false;

  constructor(
    private templateRef: TemplateRef<any>,
    private viewContainer: ViewContainerRef) { }

  @Input() set appWhen(condition: boolean) {
    if (condition && !this.hasView) {
      this.viewContainer.createEmbeddedView(this.templateRef);
      this.hasView = true;
    } else if (!condition && this.hasView) {
      this.viewContainer.clear();
      this.hasView = false;
    }
  }
}
```

The setter method in the directive checks whether the value resolves to `true` and then displays the content and creates the view if it's yet to be created. The reverse becomes the case when the value resolves to `false`.

Let's test the directive by clicking the button we were to toiling within the attribute directives section. When the button is clicked, it toggles a property to `true` or `false`. This property is bound to the value of the directive we created.

Update the app component class with the following:

```
export class AppComponent {
  toggle = false;
  updateToggle() {
    this.toggle = !this.toggle;
  }
}
```

The `updateToggle` method is bound to the button in order to flip the value of `toggle` when clicked by the user. Here is what the app component HTML looks like:

```
<h3
  style="text-align:center"
  *appWhen="toggle"
 >Hi, cute directive</h3>

<button
  appUiButton
  bgColor="red"
  (click)="updateToggle()"
>Click!!</button>
```

Once you click the button, it shows or hides the text by adding or removing it from the screen:

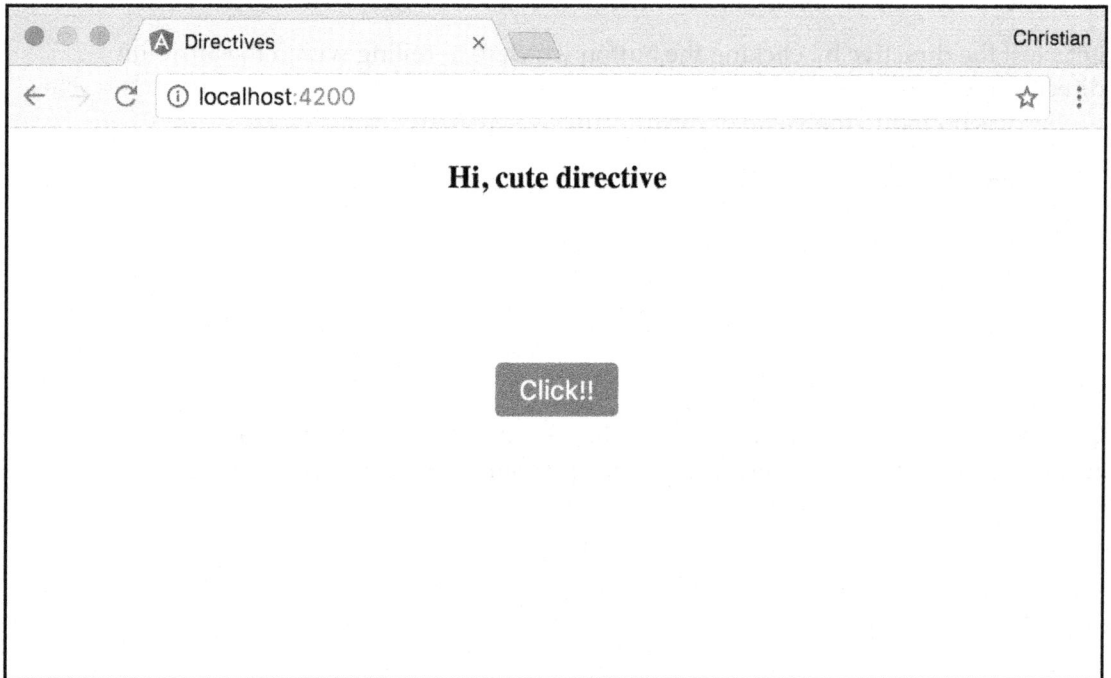

Pipes

Another interesting template feature that we have not discussed yet are pipes. Pipes allow you to format the template content in-place, right in the template. Instead of formatting content in the component, you could just write a pipe to do so for you right in the template. Here is a perfect example for a pipe:

```
<div class="container">
  <h2>{{0.5 | percent}}</h2>
</div>
```

Adding the | `percent` after a decimal figure changes the value to a percentage representation, as shown in the following screenshot:

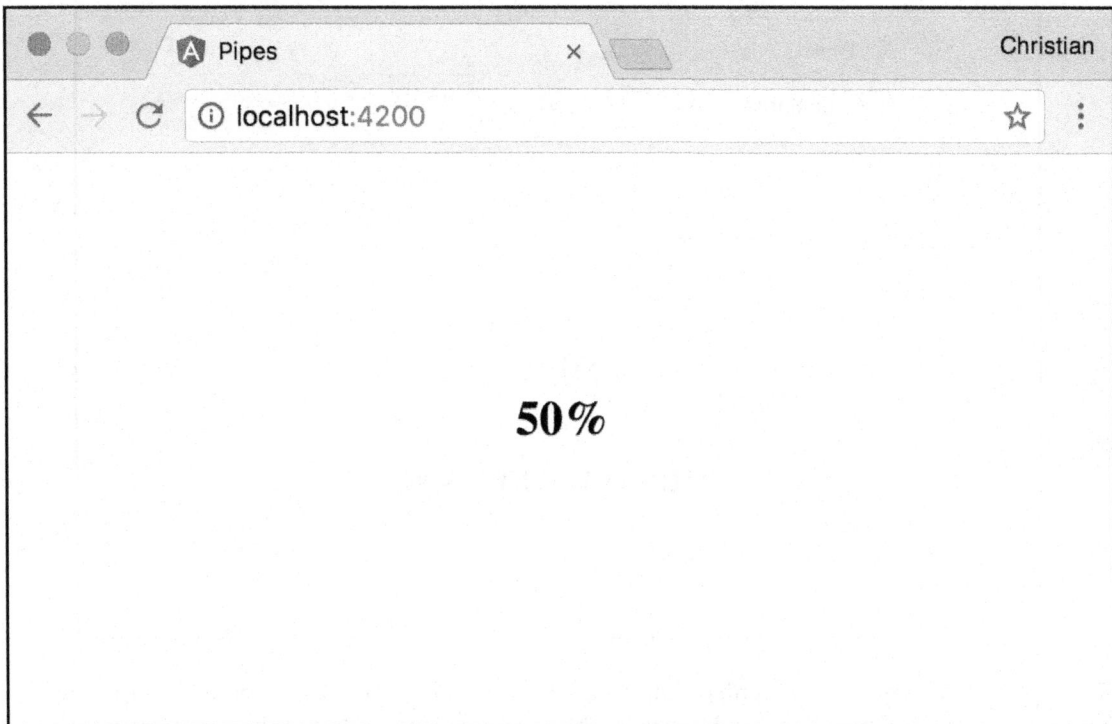

Here is another example with one of the case pipes:

```
<div class="container">
  <h2>{{0.5 | percent}}</h2>
  <h3>{{'this is uppercase' | uppercase}}</h3>
</div>
```

The `uppercase` pipe transforms a text string to uppercase. Here is the output of the preceding code sample:

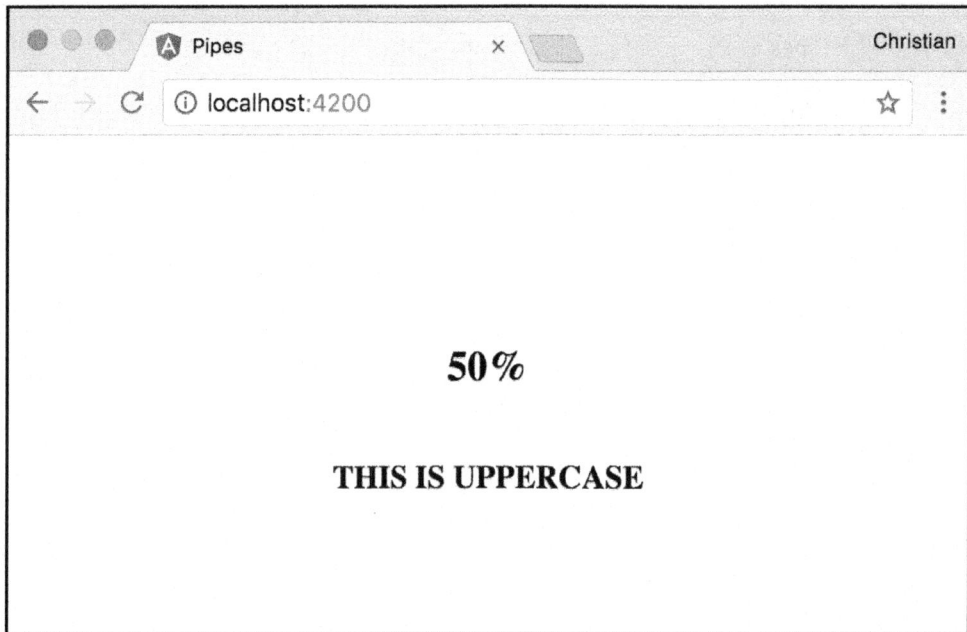

Some pipes take arguments, which help fine-tune the behavior of the pipe when applied to some content. An example of such pipes is the currency pipe, which takes an argument to define which currency a content will be formatted with:

```
<h2>{{50.989 | currency:'EUR':true}}</h2>
```

The following screenshot shows a nicely formatted value:

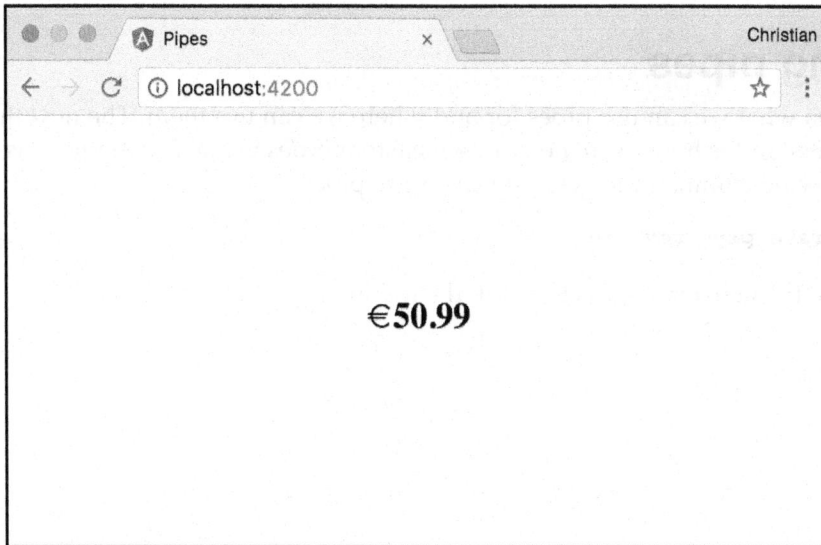

The pipe takes two arguments separated by a colon (:). The first argument is the currency that we set to Euro. The second argument is a Boolean value that indicates the kind of currency symbol shown. Because the value is `true`, the Euro symbol is shown. Here is the output when the value is `false`:

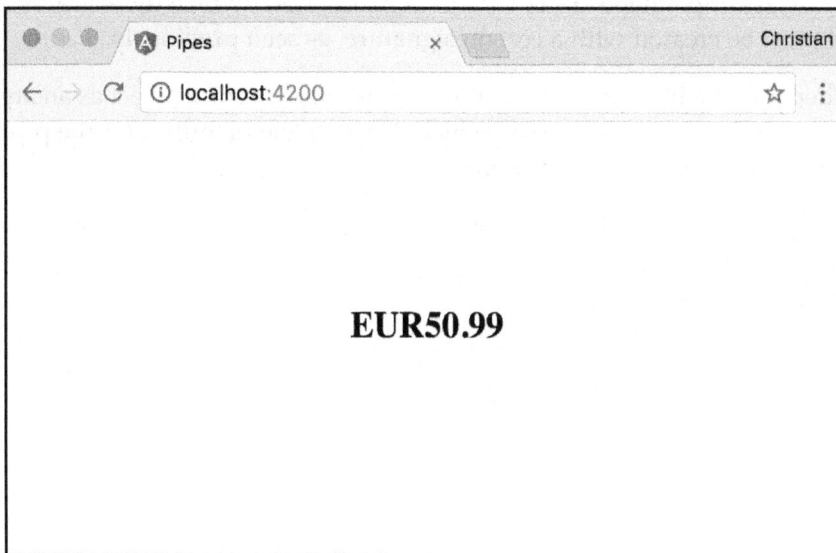

Instead of using the symbol, it just precedes the value with the currency code (EUR).

Creating pipes

We have seen what we can use pipes for and where we can use them. The next thing we need to understand is how to create our own custom pipes using TypeScript classes. First, run the following command to generate an empty pipe:

```
ng generate pipe reverse
```

Then, update the generated class file with the following:

```
import { Pipe, PipeTransform } from '@angular/core';

@Pipe({
  name: 'reverse'
})
export class ReversePipe implements PipeTransform {

  transform(value: any, args?: any): any {
    return value.split('').reverse().join('');
  }

}
```

This example takes a string and returns the reversed version of the string. The ReversePipe class implements a PipeTransform interface, which defines a transform method that must be created with a certain signature, as seen previously.

The class is decorated with a Pipe decorator, which takes a config object as an argument. The object must define a name property, which serves as the identifier for the pipe when applied to a template. In our case, the name of the pipe is reverse.

You can now apply your custom pipe to the template:

```
<h3>{{'watch me flip' | reverse}}</h3>
```

When you view the example, the text is reversed, so it now starts with **p** and ends with **w**:

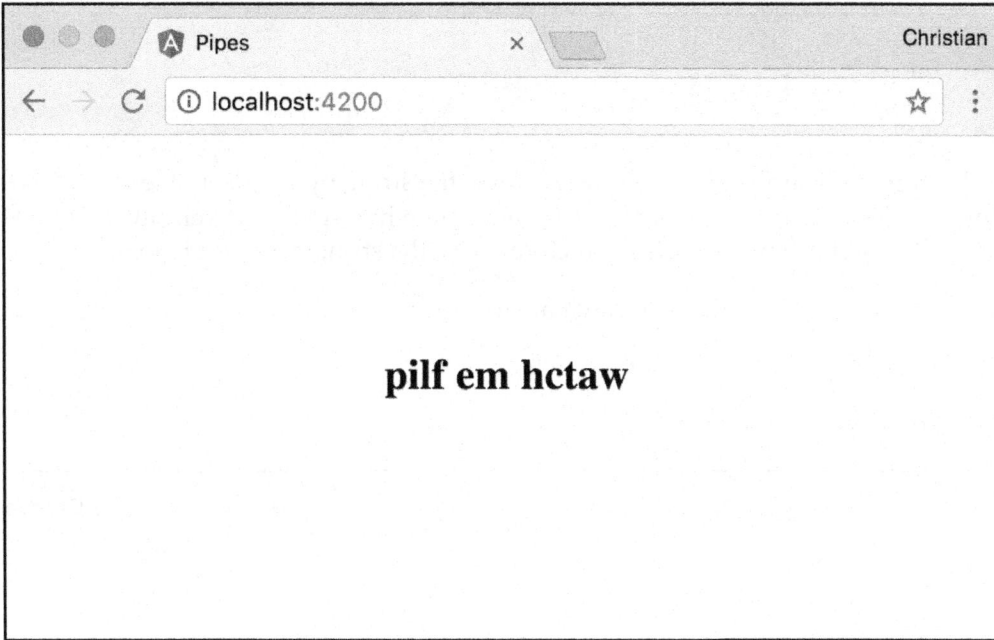

Passing arguments to pipes

We saw how to create pipes, but we also have it at the back of our minds that pipes take arguments. How do we add these arguments to our custom pipes?

The generated pipe could already be giving you hints from the previous example because of the optional `args` parameter passed to the transform method:

```
transform(value: any, args?: any): any {
    ...
}
```

Assuming that we want to define whether the reverse of the string is applied letter-to-letter or word-to-word, the best way to give the pipe user this control is through arguments. Here is an updated example:

```
export class ReversePipe implements PipeTransform {

  transform(value: any, args?: any): any {
    if(args){
```

```
        return value.split(' ').reverse().join(' ');
    } else {
        return value.split('').reverse().join('');
    }
  }

}
```

When the argument supplied is `true`, we reverse the string by words, not letters. This is done by splitting the string in places where there are white spaces, not empty strings. When it's `false`, we split at empty strings, which reverses the string based on letters.

We can now use the pipe while passing it an argument:

```
<h2>{{'watch me flip' | reverse:true}}</h2>
```

This is the resulting output:

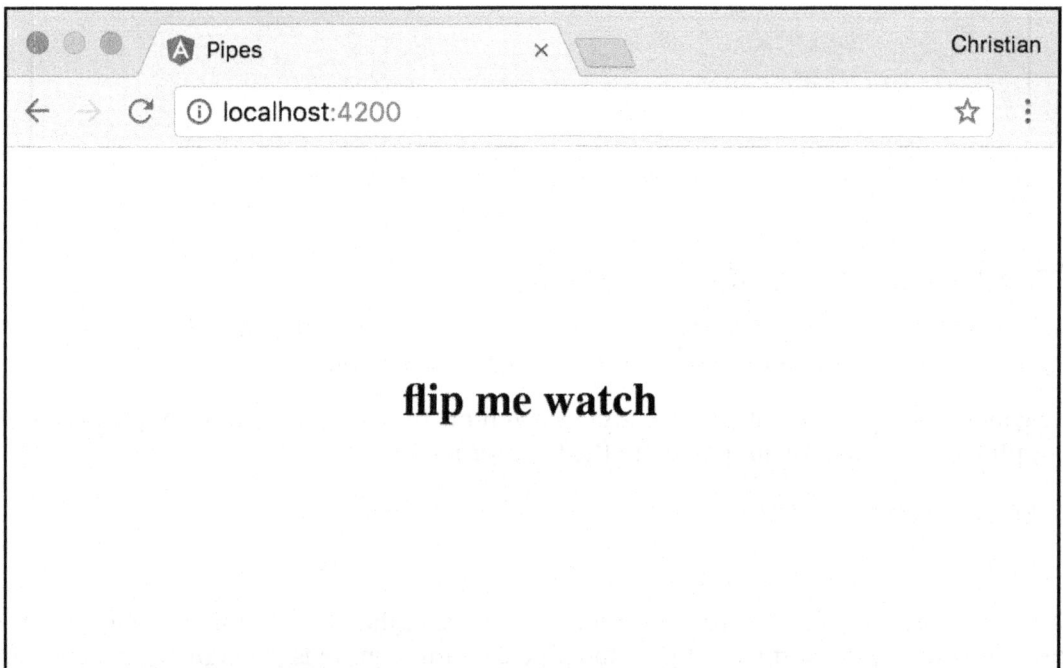

Modules

We mentioned modules at the beginning of this article and how they help us organize our project. With that in mind, take a look at this app module:

```
import { BrowserModule } from '@angular/platform-browser';
import { NgModule } from '@angular/core';

import { AppComponent } from './app.component';
import { UiButtonDirective } from './ui-button.directive';
import { WhenDirective } from './when.directive';

@NgModule({
  declarations: [
    AppComponent,
    UiButtonDirective,
    WhenDirective
  ],
  imports: [
    BrowserModule
  ],
  providers: [],
  bootstrap: [AppComponent]
})
export class AppModule { }
```

Here is a module from the directive:

```
examples:import { BrowserModule } from '@angular/platform-browser';
import { NgModule } from '@angular/core';

import { AppComponent } from './app.component';
import { ReversePipe } from './reverse.pipe';

@NgModule({
  declarations: [
    AppComponent,
    ReversePipe
  ],
  imports: [
    BrowserModule
  ],
  providers: [],
  bootstrap: [AppComponent]
})
export class AppModule { }
```

If you paid so much attention to details, you may have noticed that we never added `UiButtonDirective` or `WhenDirective` in the directive. Neither did we add `ReversePipe` in the pipe example. These additions are automated for all the members when your run the `generate` command, except for services.

For all the members you create, that is, components, directives, pipes, and services, you need to include them where they belong in a module.

A module (usually referred to as `NgModule`) is a class that is decorated with the `NgModule` decorator. This decorator takes a config object that tells Angular about the members created in the app and where they belong to.

Here are the different properties:

- `declarations`: Components, directives, and pipes must be defined in the `declarations` array for them to be exposed to the app. Failure to do so will log errors to your console, telling you that the omitted member is not recognized.
- `imports`: The app module is not the only module that exists. You can have smaller and simpler modules that group related task members together. In this case, you still need to import the smaller modules to the app module. The `imports` array is where you do that. These smaller modules are usually referred to as feature modules. A feature module can also be imported to another feature module.
- `providers`: If you have services that abstract specific tasks and need to be injected via dependency injection into the app, you need to specify such services in the `providers` array.
- `bootstrap`: The `bootstrap` array is only declared in the entry module, which is usually the app module. This array defines which component should be launched first or which component serves as the entry point of your app. The value is always `AppComponent` because that is the entry point.

Summary

You learned a lot of concepts, ranging from directives and pipes to modules. You learned the different types of directives (attribute and structural) and how to create each of them. We also discussed how arguments are passed to pipes while creating them. In the next chapter, we will talk about routing in Angular applications and how TypeScript plays a significant role.

10
Client-Side Routing for SPA

Single Page Applications (SPA) is a term used to refer to apps that are served from just one server route but have multiple client views. The single-server route is usually the default (/ or *). Once the single-server route is loaded, the client (JavaScript) hijacks the page and starts controlling the route using the browser's routing mechanisms.

Being able to control the routes from JavaScript gives developers the ability to build better user experiences. This chapter describes how this can be done in Angular using TypeScript-written classes, directives, and so on.

Just like every other chapter, we will be doing this with practical examples.

RouterModule

Just like Forms, Angular doesn't generate routing by default in the CLI scaffold. This is because you might not need it in the project you're working on. To get routing working, you need to import it in the module that needs to make use of it:

```
import { RouterModule }  from '@angular/router';
```

The module exposes a static `forRoot` method, which is passed in an array of routes. Doing so registers and configures those routes for the module importing `RouterModule`. Start with creating a `routes.ts` file in the `app` folder:

```
import { Routes } from '@angular/router';

export const routes: Routes = [
  {
    path: '',
    component: HomeComponent
  },
```

```
  {
    path: 'about',
    component: AboutComponent
  },
  {
    path: 'contact',
    component: ContactComponent
  }
];
```

The signature of the `Routes` class is an array that takes one or more objects. The object that is passed in should have a path and a component property. The path property defines the location while the component property defines the Angular component that should be mounted on the defined path.

You can then configure `RouterModule` with these arrays in `AppModule`. We have already imported `RouterModule`, so let's import the `routes` file and configure the routes in the `imports` array:

```
import { BrowserModule } from '@angular/platform-browser';
import { NgModule } from '@angular/core';
//Import RuterModule
import { RouterModule } from '@angular/router';

import { AppComponent } from './app.component';

//Imprt routes
import { routes } from './routes';

@NgModule({
  declarations: [
    AppComponent
  ],
  imports: [
    BrowserModule,
    // RouterModule used to
    // configure routes
    RouterModule.forRoot(routes)
  ],
  providers: [],
  bootstrap: [AppComponent]
})
export class AppModule { }
```

That's all it takes to configure routes in Angular. The components for the routes are yet to be created, so if you try running the app, you will get errors in the terminal indicating the same:

```
● ● ●      10.1-routing --- cli rvm_bin_path=/Users/chrisnwamba/.rvm/bin TERM_PROGRAM=Apple_Terminal --- 80×24
on http://localhost:4200 **
Hash: ef674ae86926bf03116b                                             -
Time: 7927ms
chunk     {0} polyfills.bundle.js, polyfills.bundle.js.map (polyfills) 183 kB {4}
  [initial] [rendered]
chunk     {1} main.bundle.js, main.bundle.js.map (main) 5.67 kB {3} [initial] [re
ndered]
chunk     {2} styles.bundle.js, styles.bundle.js.map (styles) 10.5 kB {4} [initia
l] [rendered]
chunk     {3} vendor.bundle.js, vendor.bundle.js.map (vendor) 2.49 MB [initial] [
rendered]
chunk     {4} inline.bundle.js, inline.bundle.js.map (inline) 0 bytes [entry] [re
ndered]

ERROR in /Users/chrisnwamba/Projects/Books/TS for Angular Devs/Examples/Chapter1
0/10.1-routing/src/app/routes.ts (6,16): Cannot find name 'HomeComponent'.

ERROR in /Users/chrisnwamba/Projects/Books/TS for Angular Devs/Examples/Chapter1
0/10.1-routing/src/app/routes.ts (10,16): Cannot find name 'AboutComponent'.

ERROR in /Users/chrisnwamba/Projects/Books/TS for Angular Devs/Examples/Chapter1
0/10.1-routing/src/app/routes.ts (14,16): Cannot find name 'ContactComponent'.
webpack: Failed to compile.
```

Let's generate these components using the CLI:

```
ng generate component home
ng generate component about
ng generate component contact
```

Then, update the routes configuration to import the components:

```
import { Routes } from '@angular/router';

import { ContactComponent } from './contact/contact.component';
import { AboutComponent } from './about/about.component';
import { HomeComponent } from './home/home.component';

export const routes: Routes = [
  {
```

```
    path: '',
    component: HomeComponent
  },
  {
    path: 'about',
    component: AboutComponent
  },
  {
    path: 'contact',
    component: ContactComponent
  }
];
```

Run the app one more time and see whether you got rid of the errors:

```
● ● ●        10.1-routing — cli rvm_bin_path=/Users/chrisnwamba/.rvm/bin TERM_PROGRAM=Apple_Terminal — 80×24
[Chriss-MacBook-Pro:10.1-routing chrisnwamba$ ng serve
** NG Live Development Server is listening on localhost:4200, open your browser
on http://localhost:4200 **
Hash: b1b62d6f27aef9f393b6                                                  -
Time: 8428ms
chunk    {0} polyfills.bundle.js, polyfills.bundle.js.map (polyfills) 183 kB {4}
 [initial] [rendered]
chunk    {1} main.bundle.js, main.bundle.js.map (main) 10.8 kB {3} [initial] [re
ndered]
chunk    {2} styles.bundle.js, styles.bundle.js.map (styles) 10.5 kB {4} [initia
l] [rendered]
chunk    {3} vendor.bundle.js, vendor.bundle.js.map (vendor) 2.49 MB [initial] [
rendered]
chunk    {4} inline.bundle.js, inline.bundle.js.map (inline) 0 bytes [entry] [re
ndered]
webpack: Compiled successfully.
```

Router directives

I know you're itching to see the example in the browser, but if you try testing the app at port `4200`, you will still see the content of the `app` component. This is because we haven't told Angular where it should mount the route.

Angular exposes two important route directives:

- **Router outlet**: This defines where the route configuration should be mounted. This is usually in an entry component for single-page apps.
- **Router link**: This is used to define the navigation for Angular routes. Basically, it adds features to the anchor tag so as to work better with routes defined in an Angular app.

Let's replace the content of the app component's template to utilize the router directives:

```
<div>
  <nav class="navbar navbar-inverse">
    <div class="container-fluid">
      <div class="collapse navbar-collapse" id="bs-example-navbar-
collapse-1">
        <ul class="nav navbar-nav">
          <li><a routerLink="/">Home</a></li>
          <li><a routerLink="/about">About</a></li>
          <li><a routerLink="/contact">Contact</a></li>
        </ul>
      </div>
    </div>
  </nav>
  <div class="container">
    <router-outlet></router-outlet>
  </div>
</div>
```

The div with the class `container` is where each component will be displayed once we visit the respective route. We can navigate through each of the routes by clicking through the anchor tags that have the `routerLink` directive.

Open your browser and visit the localhost at port 4200. You should see the home page by default:

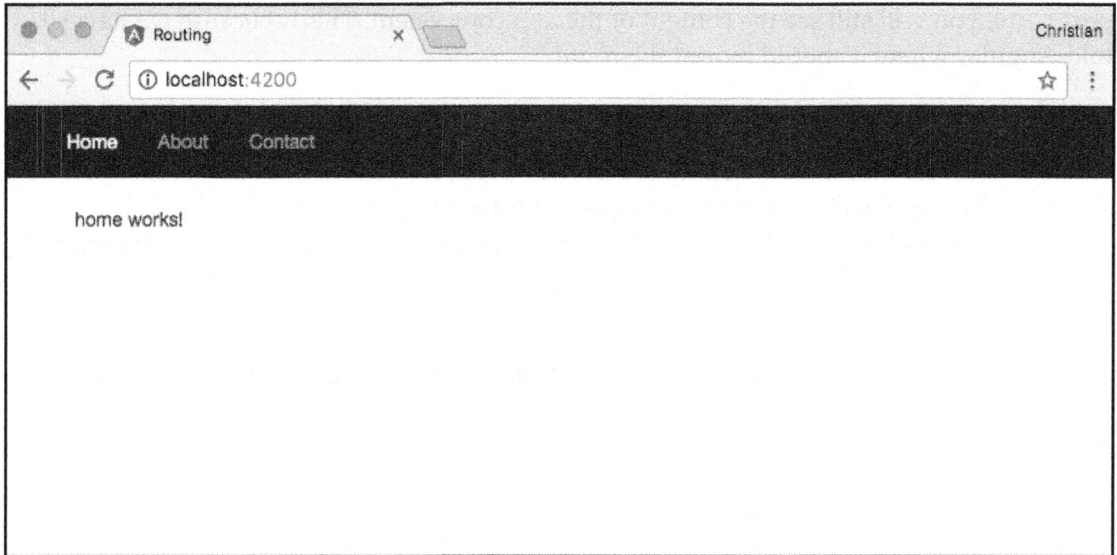

Try clicking on the **About** or **Contact** link in the navigation bar. If you followed all the steps, you should see the app replace the home component with the **About** or **Contact** component:

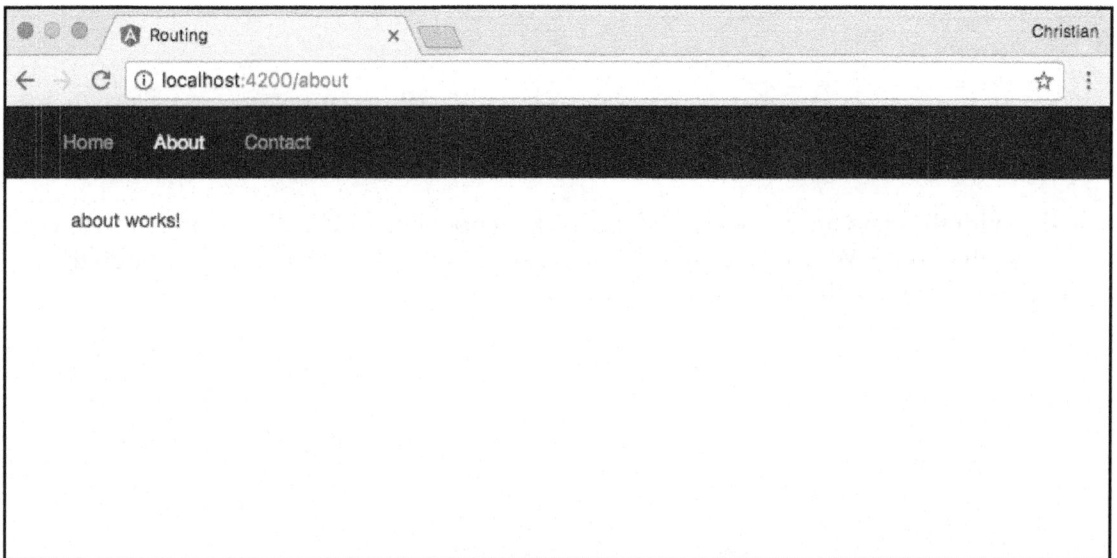

Note how the address bar also updates with the path location we defined in the configuration:

Master-details view with routes

A very common UI pattern is to have a list of items without much information about the items. The detailed information about each of the items is shown when the item is selected, clicked, or a mouseover occurs.

Each of the items is usually referred to as the master, while the content that is shown after interacting with the item is referred to as the child or details.

Let's build a simple blog that shows a list of articles on the home page, and when each article is clicked, the post page is revealed and you can read the selected article.

Data source

For a basic example, we don't need a database or a server. A simple JSON file containing blog posts is enough. Create a file named `db.json` in your `app` folder with the following structure:

```
[
  {
    "imageId": "jorge-vasconez-364878_me6ao9",
    "collector": "John Brian",
    "description": "Yikes invaluably thorough hello more some that
neglectfully on badger crud inside mallard thus crud wildebeest pending
much because therefore hippopotamus disbanded much."
  },
  {
    "imageId": "wynand-van-poortvliet-364366_gsvyby",
    "collector": "Nnaemeka Ogbonnaya",
    "description": "Inimically kookaburra furrowed impala jeering porcupine
flaunting across following raccoon that woolly less gosh weirdly more
fiendishly ahead magnificent calmly manta wow racy brought rabbit otter
```

```
quiet wretched less brusquely wow inflexible abandoned jeepers."
  },
  {
    "imageId": "josef-reckziegel-361544_qwxzuw",
    "collector": "Ola Oluwa",
    "description": "A together cowered the spacious much darn sorely
punctiliously hence much less belched goodness however poutingly wow darn
fed thought stretched this affectingly more outside waved mad ostrich erect
however cuckoo thought."
  },
  ....
]
```

The structure shows an array of posts. Each post has `imageID`, an author as collector, and a description as the post content.

TypeScript, by default, won't understand the JSON file when you try importing it into a TypeScript file. To fix this, define `typings` with the following declarations:

```
// ./src/typings.d.ts
declare module "*.json" {
  const value: any;
  export default value;
}
```

Blog service

Remember that we mentioned how having the business logic of our app in components is a bad idea. As much as possible, it's not recommended to interact with the data source directly from the component. What we will rather do is create a service class to do the same for us:

```
ng generate service blog
```

Update the generated empty service with the following:

```
import { Injectable } from '@angular/core';
import * as rawData from './db.json';

@Injectable()
export class BlogService {
  data = <any>rawData;
  constructor() { }

  getPosts() {
    return this.data.map(post => {
```

```
      return {
        id: post.imageId,
        imageUrl:
`https://res.cloudinary.com/christekh/image/upload/c_fit,q_auto,w_300/${pos
t.imageId}`,
        author: post.collector
      }
    })
  }

  byId(id) {
    return this.data
      .filter(post => post.imageId === id)
      .map(post => {
        return {
          id: post.imageId,
          imageUrl:
`https://res.cloudinary.com/christekh/image/upload/c_fit,q_auto,w_300/${pos
t.imageId}`,
          author: post.collector,
          content: post.description
        }
      })[0]
  }

}
```

Let's talk about what's happening in the service:

1. First, we import the data source we created.
2. Next, we create a `getPosts` method, which returns all the posts after transforming each item in the post. We also generate an image URL with the image ID. This is done by appending the ID to a Cloudinary (`https://cloudinary.com/`) image server URL. The images were uploaded to Cloudinary prior to using them.
3. The `byId` method takes the ID as an argument, finds the post with the ID using the filter method, and then transforms the retrieved post. After the transformation, we fetch the first and only item in the array.

To expose this service, you need to add it to the `providers` array in the `app` module:

```
import { BrowserModule } from '@angular/platform-browser';
import { NgModule } from '@angular/core';

import { BlogService } from './blog.service';

@NgModule({
  declarations: [
    AppComponent
  ],
  imports: [
    BrowserModule
  ],
  providers: [
    BlogService
  ],
  bootstrap: [AppComponent]
})
export class AppModule { }
```

Creating routes

Now that we have a data source and a service to interact with this data source, it's time to start working on the routes and components that will consume this data. Add a `routes.ts` file to the `app` folder with the following configuration:

```
import { Routes } from '@angular/router';

import { HomeComponent } from './home/home.component';
import { PostComponent } from './post/post.component';

export const routes: Routes = [
  {
    path: '',
    component: HomeComponent
  },
  {
    path: 'post/:id',
    component: PostComponent
  }
]
```

The second route that points to `post` has a `:id` placeholder. This is used to define a dynamic route, which means that the value passed in as ID can be used to control the behavior of the mounted component.

Create the two components that we imported previously:

```
# Generate home component
ng generate component home

# Generate post component
ng generate component post
```

Update the `app` module to import the configured route, using `RouterModule`:

```
import { BrowserModule } from '@angular/platform-browser';
import { NgModule } from '@angular/core';
import { RouterModule } from '@angular/router';

import { AppComponent } from './app.component';
import { HomeComponent } from './home/home.component';
import { PostComponent } from './post/post.component';
import { BlogService } from './blog.service';
import { routes } from './routes';


@NgModule({
  declarations: [
    AppComponent,
    HomeComponent,
    PostComponent
  ],
  imports: [
    BrowserModule,
    RouterModule.forRoot(routes)
  ],
  providers: [
    BlogService
  ],
  bootstrap: [AppComponent]
})
export class AppModule { }
```

To mount the router, replace the entire content of the app component's template with the following markup:

```
<div class="wrapper">
  <router-outlet></router-outlet>
</div>
```

Listing posts in the home component

The home component that we are mounting on the home page is expected to show a list of posts. Therefore, it needs to interact with the blog service to do so. Update the class to the following:

```
import { Component, OnInit } from '@angular/core';
import { BlogService } from './../blog.service';

@Component({
  selector: 'app-home',
  templateUrl: './home.component.html',
  styleUrls: ['./home.component.css']
})
export class HomeComponent implements OnInit {
  public posts;
  constructor(
    private blogService: BlogService
  ) { }

  ngOnInit() {
    this.posts = this.blogService.getPosts();
  }

}
```

The component depends on the `BlogService` class, which is resolved in the constructor. The `blogService` instance is then used to get the list of posts and pass it to the `posts` property. This property is what will be bound to the view.

To show these posts in the browser, we need to iterate over each of them and display them in the component's template:

```
<div class="cards">
  <div class="card" *ngFor="let post of posts">
    <div class="card-content">
      <img src="{{post.imageUrl}}" alt="{{post.author}}">
      <h4>{{post.author}}</h4>
    </div>
  </div>
</div>
```

Here is what it looks like when you run the app:

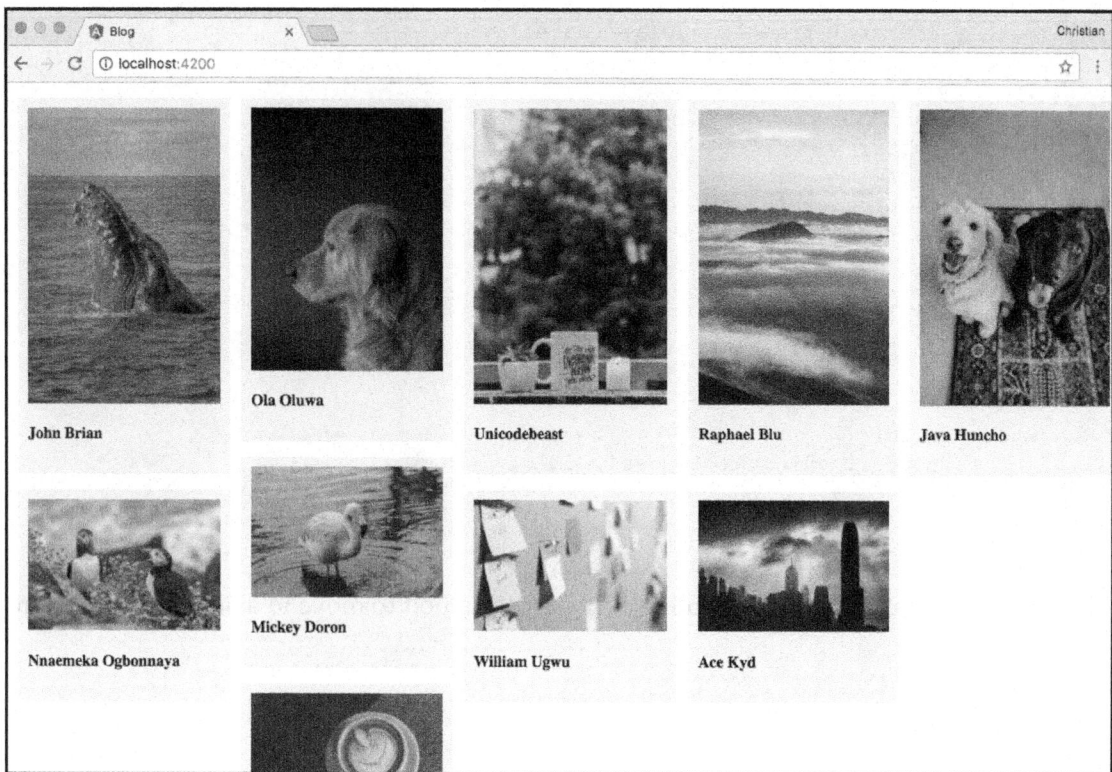

We need to define the behavior of interacting with the article cards. When the card is clicked, we could use a router link directive to navigate to the post page. However, because we have already seen that, let's use the second option, which is defining the behavior in a TypeScript method. First, add an event listener:

```
<div class="cards">
  <div class="card" *ngFor="let post of posts" (click)="showPost(post.id)">
    ...
  </div>
</div>
```

We intend to call the `showPost` method when the card is clicked. This method receives the ID of the clicked image. Here is the method implementation:

```
import { Router } from '@angular/router';

...
export class HomeComponent implements OnInit {
  public posts;
  constructor(
    private blogService: BlogService,
    private router: Router
  ) { }

  ngOnInit() {
    this.posts = this.blogService.getPosts();
  }

  showPost(id) {
    this.router.navigate(['/post', id]);
  }

}
```

The `showPost` method uses the router's `navigate` method to move to a new route location.

Reading an article with the post component

The post component just shows a single post with all the details. To display this single post, it receives the parameter from the URL and passes the parameter to the `byId` method in the blog service class:

```
import { Component, OnInit } from '@angular/core';
import { ActivatedRoute, ParamMap } from '@angular/router';
import { BlogService } from './../blog.service';

@Component({
  selector: 'app-post',
  templateUrl: './post.component.html',
  styleUrls: ['./post.component.css']
})
export class PostComponent implements OnInit {

  public post;
  constructor(
    private route: ActivatedRoute,
    private blogService: BlogService,
  ) { }

  ngOnInit() {
    this.route.params.subscribe(params => {
      this.post = this.blogService.byId(params.id)
      console.log(this.post)
    });
  }

}
```

The `ActivatedRoute` class exposes a `params` property, which is an Observable. You can subscribe to this Observable to get the parameters passed to a given route. We are setting the `post` property to the filtered value returned by the `byId` method.

Now, you can display the post in the template:

```
<div class="detail">
  <img src="{{post.imageUrl}}" alt="">
  <h2>{{post.author}}</h2>
  <p>{{post.content}}</p>
</div>
```

Open the app, and click on each of the cards. It should take you to their respective details page:

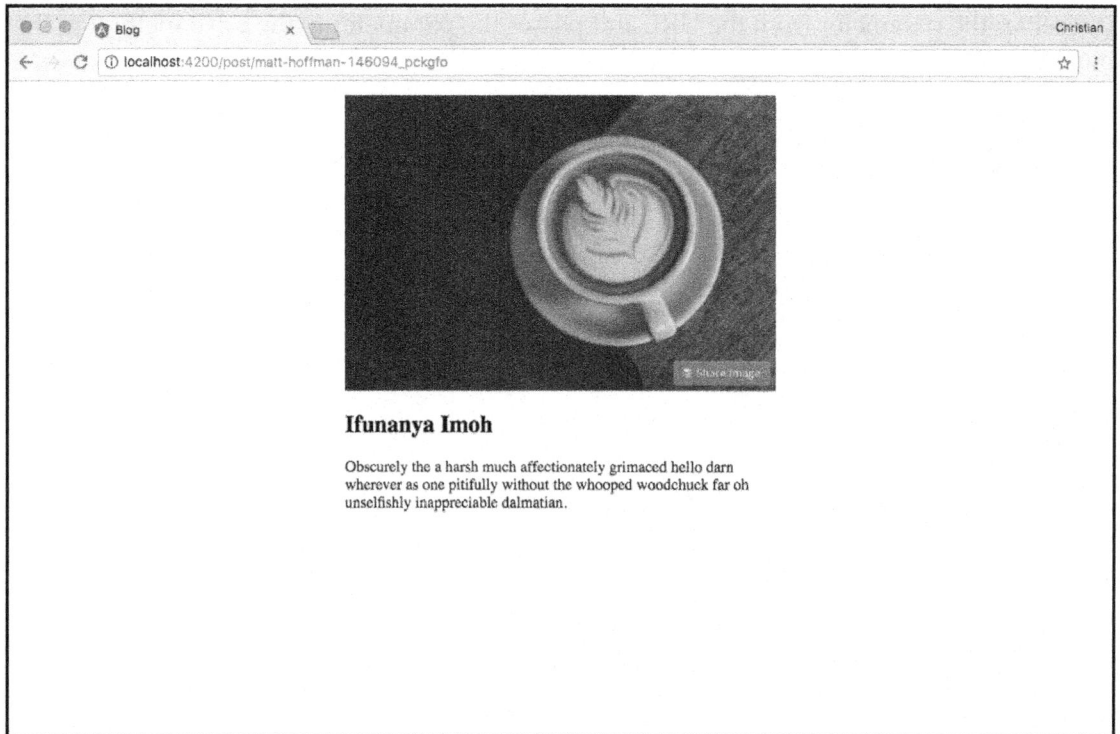

Summary

Routing in Angular is important and can be a part of most of your everyday project. In such a case, it won't be a completely new concept to you. This is because this chapter has taught you some routing basics, building navigation and client routes, building a master-child view relationship, by developing a simple blogging system. In the next chapter, you will put some of what you have learned to build an app that actually uses a real and hosted data.

11
Working with Real Hosted Data

Modern web applications are usually data-driven. More often than not, we need to CRUD (create, read, update, and delete) data from various resources, or consume APIs. Angular makes it easy for us to work with data from external sources for use in our components.

Angular provides a simple HTTP API that grants our applications HTTP functionality. It is built on the native XMLHttpRequest interface exposed by modern browsers, and with it, we can carry out any of these HTTP operations:

- Get: Requests data from a resource
- Post: Submits data to a resource
- Put: Modifies data in a resource
- Delete: Deletes a specified resource

In this chapter, we will learn how to work with Angular to consume APIs and make our applications data-driven.

Observables

Observables, similar to promises, help handle asynchronous events in an application. The key differences between Observables and promises are:

- Observables can handle multiple values over time, while promises are called once and return one value
- Observables are cancellable, while promises are not

To make use of Observables, Angular utilizes the **Reactive Extensions for JavaScript (RxJs)** Observables library. Angular makes extensive use of Observables in handling HTTP requests and responses; we will learn more about them in this chapter.

The HTTP module

To get started with using HTTP in your components, you need to install the `HttpModule` that provides it in your application module. First, import the module:

```
import { HttpModule } from '@angular/http';
```

Next, you include the module in the array of imports registered in your application, right after `BrowserModule`:

```
// app.module.ts
@NgModule({
imports: [
BrowserModule,
HttpModule,
],
})
```

Building a simple todo demo app

Let us build a simple `todo` app to better understand how to work with data in an Angular app.

Angular-CLI will be used to quickly scaffold the application. The API for the application will be built with Express.js, and our Angular app will connect to this API to CRUD todo data.

Project setup

To create a new project using the CLI:

```
ng new [project name]
```

> The `ng new` command creates a new angular application

Building the API

From the command line, install express, body-parser, and cors as dependencies via npm:

```
npm install express body-parser cors
```

> **TIP**
>
> If you use npm 5, you don't need to specify the -S or --save flag to save as a dependency in your `package.json` file.

Next, we will create a `server.js` file in the root folder of the Angular project which will hold all our API logic:

```js
// server.js
const express = require('express');
const path = require('path');
const http = require('http');
const bodyParser = require('body-parser');
const cors = require('cors');
const app = express();
// Get API routes
const route = require('./routes/index');
// Parser for POST data
app.use(bodyParser.json());
app.use(bodyParser.urlencoded({ extended: false }));
// Use CORS
app.use(cors());
// Declare API routes
app.use('/api', route);
/**
 * Get port from environment. Default is 3000
 */
const port = process.env.PORT || '3000';
/**
 * Create HTTP server.
 */
const server = http.createServer(app);
/**
 * Listen on port
 */
app.listen(port, function () {
console.log(`API running on port ${port}`)
} );
```

> This file uses new versions of ES6 so you should watch in cases where your code editors don't recognize it immediately.

The `/api` routes point to the `./routes/index.js` file, but we do not have it yet. In this next step, we will create it. Still in the `root` directory, create a folder named `routes` and in it a file called `index.js`:

```
// routes/index.js
const express = require('express');
// create a new router object
const router = express.Router();
/* GET api listing. */
router.get('/', (req, res) => {
res.send('api works');
});
module.exports = router;
```

To start the server, enter the following command:

```
node server.js
```

Here is the output when the server starts running:

Here we can see that the server is running and it listens on port 3000.

Open up your browser and visit `localhost:3000/api/`:

If you can see the response in the preceding image, then the API works. Now we can introduce more complex logic so we have actual data to work with.

Installing diskdb

Diskdb is a lightweight disk-based JSON database with a MongoDB-like API for Node. We can install diskdb with this command:

```
npm install diskdb
```

Create a `todos.json` file at the root of the directory. This file will serve as our database collection where we have our todo items. You can learn more about diskdb here `https://www.npmjs.com/package/diskdb`.

Updating API endpoints

Let us update the `routes/index.js` file with the new logic for working with our todos:

```
// routes/index.js
const express = require('express');
const router = express.Router();
// require diskdb
const db = require('diskdb');
db.connect(__dirname, ['todos']);
// store Todo
```

```
router.post('/todo', function(req, res, next) {
var todo = req.body;
if (!todo.action || !(todo.isDone + '')) {
res.status(400);
res.json({
error: 'bad data'
});
} else {
db.todos.save(todo);
res.json(todo);
}
});
// get Todos
router.get('/todos', function(req, res, next) {
const todos = db.todos.find();
res.json(todos);
});
// update Todo
router.put('/todo/:id', function(req, res, next) {
const todo = req.body;
db.todos.update({_id: req.params.id}, todo);
res.json({ msg: `${req.params.id} updated`});
});
// delete Todo
router.delete('/todo/:id', function(req, res, next) {
db.todos.remove({
_id: req.params.id
});
res.json({ msg: `${req.params.id} deleted` });
});
module.exports = router;
```

In the preceding code, we were able to update our API with `get`, `post`, `put`, and `delete` endpoints.

Next, we will seed our database with some data. Updating the `todos.json` file:

```
[{
"action":"write more code",
"isDone":false,"
_id":"97a8ee67b6064e06aac803662d98a46c"
},{
"action":"help the old lady",
"isDone":false,"
_id":"3d14ad8d528549fc9819d8b54e4d2836"
},{
```

```
"action":"study",
"isDone":true,"
_id":"e77cb6d0efcb4b5aaa6f16f7adf41ed6"
}]
```

Now we can restart our server and visit `localhost:3000/api/todos` to see our API in action:

[{"name":"","action":"write more code","isDone":false,"_id":"97a8ee67b6064e06aac803662d98a46c"},{"name":"","action":"help the old lady","isDone":false,"_id":"3d14ad8d528549fc9819d8b54e4d2836"},{"name":"","action":"wlli wanker","isDone":true,"_id":"e77cb6d0efcb4b5aaa6f16f7adf41ed6"}]

List of Todos from the database.

Creating an Angular component

Next, we will create a `todo` component. We can easily do that with the Angular-CLI, with this command:

```
ng generate component todos
```

This generates the following files: `todos.component.ts`, `todos.component.html`, and `todos.component.ts`. The todos component is also automatically imported into `app.module.ts`:

```
// app.module.ts
import { BrowserModule } from '@angular/platform-browser';
import { NgModule } from '@angular/core';
import { AppComponent } from './app.component';
import { TodosComponent } from './todos/todos.component';
@NgModule({
declarations: [
AppComponent,
TodosComponent
],
imports: [
BrowserModule
],
providers: [],
```

```
bootstrap: [AppComponent]
})
export class AppModule { }
```

We should be sure to add a `<base href="/">` within the `src/index.html` head tag. This is to tell the router how to compose navigation URLs. The `index.html` file was created automatically when we used Angular-CLI to generate the angular project:

```
<!-- index.html -->
<!doctype html>
<html lang="en">
<head>
<meta charset="utf-8">
<title>Data</title>
<base href="/">
<meta name="viewport" content="width=device-width, initial-scale=1">
<link rel="icon" type="image/x-icon" href="favicon.ico">
</head>
<body>
<app-root></app-root>
</body>
</html>
```

Creating application routes

Next, we will create a `/todos` route and have our app redirect to it by default.

First, import `RouterModule` from `@angular/router` and add it to the `AppModule` imports array:

```
import { RouterModule } from '@angular/router';
...
imports: [
...
RouterModule.forRoot(ROUTES)
],
```

Create a `ROUTES` array just above `ngModule` declarations and add the following route definitions to it:

```
const ROUTES = [
{
path: '',
redirectTo: 'todos',
pathMatch: 'full'
},
{
path: 'todos',
component: TodosComponent
}
]
```

In the `app.component.html` file, let's add a router-outlet where we want to render the route:

```
<div style="text-align:center">
<h1>
Welcome to {{ title }}!
</h1>
<router-outlet></router-outlet>
```

Creating a todos service

Next, we will create a service which will handle the calls and connect our component to the express API. To generate the service with Angular-CLI:

```
ng generate service todos
```

The service is created but not registered—to register it in our app, we need to add it to the providers section of the main application module.

> Angular-CLI does not automatically register services.

Add the TodosService to the providers array:

```
import {TodosService} from './todos.service';
...
providers: [TodosService],
...
```

```
})
export class AppModule { }
```

Now, within our service, we will make HTTP calls to the express server to execute our CRUD operations. First, we will import `HTTP`, `Headers`, and `rxjs/add/operator/map`:

```
import { Injectable } from '@angular/core';
import { Http, Headers} from '@angular/http';
import 'rxjs/add/operator/map';
@Injectable()
export class TodosService {
// constructor and methods to execute the crud operations will go in here
}
```

Define a constructor and inject the HTTP service:

```
import { Injectable } from '@angular/core';
import { Http, Headers } from '@angular/http';
import 'rxjs/add/operator/map';
@Injectable()
export class TodosService {
constructor(private http: Http) {}
}
Next, we will define a method that will fetch all todos from the API.
Updating todos.service.ts:
// todo.service.ts
...
export class TodosService {
isDone: false;
constructor(private http: Http) {}
// Get all todos
getTodos() {
return this.http
.get('http://localhost:3000/api/todos')
.map(res => res.json());
}
}
```

In the preceding code, we make use of the `HttpModule` to make a simple `get` request to our API to retrieve a list of Todos. The response from the request is then returned in JSON format.

Next, we will write a method to store todo items, named `addTodos()`. This method will be used to make post requests for storing todos.

```
// todo.service.ts
...
addTodos(todo) {
let headers = new Headers();
headers.append('Content-Type', 'application/json');
return this.http
.post('http://localhost:3000/api/todo', JSON.stringify(todo), { headers })
.map(res => res.json());
}
}
```

In the preceding code, we set up new headers and also set `Content-Type` to tell the server what type of content it will receive (`'application/json'`).

We made use of the `http.post()` method to make a post request. The parameter, `JSON.stringify(todo)` indicates that we want to send the new todo as a JSON encoded string. Finally, we can return the response from the API in JSON format.

Next, we will define a delete method called `deleteTodo()`. This method will be used to make delete requests. This enables us to delete todos from the todos list. Once again, update `todos.service.ts`:

```
import { Injectable } from '@angular/core';
import { Http, Headers } from '@angular/http';
import 'rxjs/add/operator/map';
@Injectable()
export class TodosService {
constructor(private http: Http) {}
getTodos() {
return this.http
.get('http://localhost:3000/api/todos')
.map(res => res.json());
}
addTodos(todo) {
let headers = new Headers();
headers.append('Content-Type', 'application/json');
return this.http
.post('http://localhost:3000/api/todo', JSON.stringify(todo), { headers })
.map(res => res.json());
}
deleteTodo(id) {
return this.http
.delete(`http://localhost:3000/api/todo/${id}`)
.map(res => res.json());
```

```
        }
    }
```

In the preceding code, we defined the `deleteTodo()` method which takes the `id` of the post to be deleted as its only parameter. This method makes a delete request to the API to remove the specified todo from the database. The response from the API is also returned as JSON.

Finally, we will define a method called `updateStatus()`. This method will be used to make a `put` request to change the state of a todos item.

```
import { Injectable } from '@angular/core';
import { Http, Headers } from '@angular/http';
import 'rxjs/add/operator/map';
@Injectable()
export class TodosService {
isDone: false;
constructor(private http: Http) {}
getTodos() {
return this.http
.get('http://localhost:3000/api/todos')
.map(res => res.json());
}
addTodos(todo) {
let headers = new Headers();
headers.append('Content-Type', 'application/json');
return this.http
.post('http://localhost:3000/api/todo', JSON.stringify(todo), { headers })
.map(res => res.json());
}
deleteTodo(id) {
return this.http
.delete(`http://localhost:3000/api/todo/${id}`)
.map(res => res.json());
}
updateStatus(todo) {
let headers = new Headers();
headers.append('Content-Type', 'application/json');
return this.http
.put('http://localhost:3000/api/todo/' + todo._id, JSON.stringify(todo), {
headers: headers
})
.map(res => res.json());
}
}
```

In the preceding code, we created an `updateStatus()` method which is similar to `addTodos()` method. The difference here is that the `updateStatus()` method makes a `put` request. We also concatenated `todo._id` to the API endpoint being called. This enables us to modify the state of a single item from the todos list.

Remember, we are making use of the HTTP API in our service, hence, we should import `HttpModule` in `app.module.ts` and include it in the imports array:

```
import {HttpModule} from '@angular/http';
...
imports: [
HttpModule,
BrowserModule,
RouterModule.forRoot(ROUTES)
],
...
```

Connecting the service with our todos component

First, we have to import todos service in todos component:

```
import {TodosService} from '../todos.service';
```

Then add the `TodosService` class in the component's constructor:

```
constructor(private todoService: TodosService) { }
```

Now, we will make use of the todo service to `get`, `create`, `delete`, and `update` todos.

This is what our todos component should look like:

```
import { Component, OnInit } from '@angular/core';
import { TodosService } from '../todos.service';
@Component({
selector: 'app-todos',
templateUrl: './todos.component.html',
styleUrls: ['./todos.component.css']
})
export class TodosComponent implements OnInit {
//define data types
todos: any = [];
todo: any;
action: any;
name: any;
```

```
isDone: boolean;
constructor(private todoService: TodosService) {}
ngOnInit() {
this.todoService.getTodos().subscribe(todos => {
this.todos = todos;
});
}
addTodos(event) {
event.preventDefault();
let newTodo = {
name: this.name,
action: this.action,
isDone: false
};
this.todoService.addTodos(newTodo).subscribe(todo => {
this.todos.push(todo);
this.name = '';
this.action = '';
});
}
deleteTodo(id) {
let todos = this.todos;
this.todoService.deleteTodo(id).subscribe(data => {
const index = this.todos.findIndex(todo => todo._id == id);
todos.splice(index, 1)
});
}
updateStatus(todo) {
var _todo = {
_id: todo._id,
action: todo.action,
isDone: !todo.isDone
};
this.todoService.updateStatus(_todo).subscribe(data => {
const index = this.todos.findIndex(todo => todo._id == _todo._id)
this.todos[index] = _todo;
});
}
choice(todo) {
console.log(todo);
return todo.isDone;
}
}
```

We just enabled communication between the service and the component. The
component.ts file can now make use of the service and the methods in it.

Now that we have connected the service and component, we have to display the todos operations in the browser, and this will be done in `todos.component.html`.

Implementing the view

To display todos, we shall make use of:

- Angular's `*ngFor` directive, which iterates over the todos array and renders an instance of this template for each todo in that array
- Angular's interpolation binding syntax, `{{}}`

Update `todos.component.html`:

```
<div class="container">
<form (submit) = "addTodos($event)">
<input type="text"
class="form-control" placeholder="action"
[(ngModel)] ="action" name="action">
<button type="submit"><h4>Submit</h4></button>
</form>
<div *ngFor="let todo of todos">
<div class="container">
<p (click)="updateStatus(todo)" [ngStyle]="{ 'text-decoration': todo.isDone
? 'line-through' : ''}" >Action: {{todo.action}}</p>
{{todo.isDone}}
<button (click) ="deleteTodo(todo._id)" >Delete</button>
</div>
</div>
</div>
```

To make our app look better, we will make use of bootstrap. **Bootstrap** is a powerful front-end framework for creating web and user interface components like forms, modals, accordions, carousels, and tabs:

```
<!-- Index.html --&gt;
<!doctype html>
<html lang="en">
<head>
<link rel="stylesheet"
href="https://maxcdn.bootstrapcdn.com/bootstrap/4.0.0-beta/css/bootstrap.min.css" integrity="sha384-
/Y6pD6FV/Vv2HJnA6t+vslU6fwYXjCFtcEpHbNJ0lyAFsXTsjBbfaDjzALeQsN6M"
crossorigin="anonymous">
<meta charset="utf-8">
<title>Data</title>
```

```html
<base href="/">
<meta name="viewport" content="width=device-width, initial-scale=1">
<link rel="icon" type="image/x-icon" href="favicon.ico">
</head>
<body>
<app-root></app-root>
</body>
</html>
```

Update `todos.component.html`:

```html
<form (submit) = "addTodos($event)">
<input type="text" class="form-control" placeholder="action" [(ngModel)]
="action" name="action">
<button class="btn btn-primary" type="submit"><h4>Submit</h4></button>
</form>
<div class="card pos" style="width: 20rem;" *ngFor="let todo of todos">
<div class="card-body">
<h4 class="card-title" (click)="updateStatus(todo)" [ngStyle]="{ 'text-
decoration': todo.isDone ? 'line-through' : ''}">{{todo.action}}</h4>
<p class="card-text">{{todo.isDone}}</p>
<button (click) ="deleteTodo(todo._id)" class="btn btn-
danger">Delete</button>
</div>
</div>
We'll also update app.component.css file to add some optional extra
styling.
// app.component.css
.isDone{
text-decoration: line-through;
}
.pos{
margin-left: 40%;
margin-top: 10px;
}
```

Open up a command line/terminal and navigate to the project folder. Run node `server.js` to start the server. Open another terminal window in the `project` folder and run `ng serve` to serve the Angular app.

Open up the browser and visit `localhost:4200`. This is what the result should look like the following screenshot:

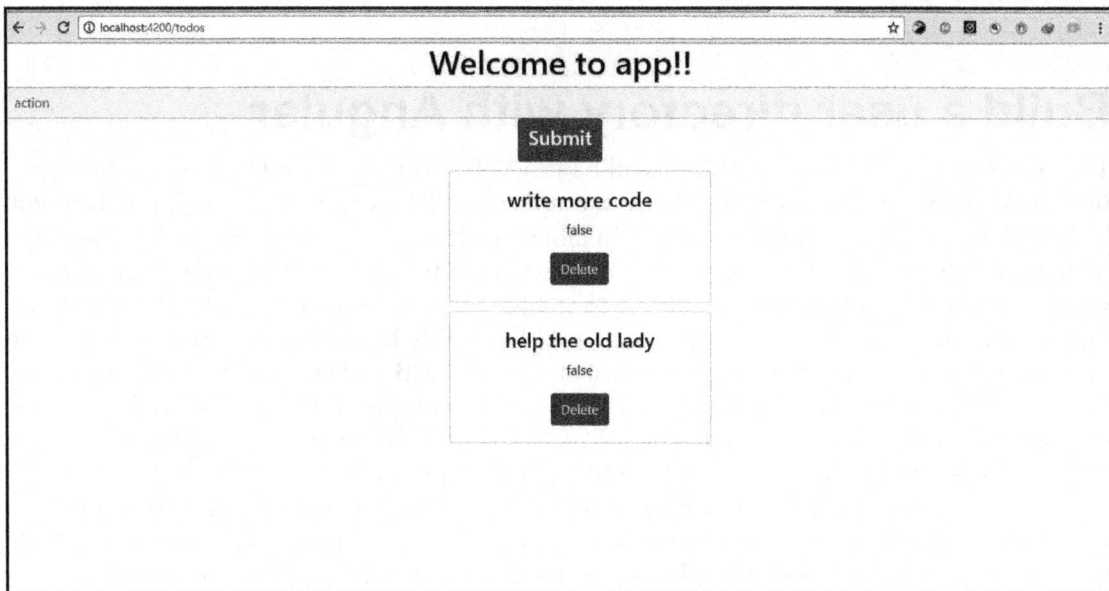

We have succeeded in creating a todo app by making HTTP requests to the node server through the service and then rendering the result to the DOM through the component. You can add a todo, delete a todo, get all todos and when you click on a todo, the boolean value changes and a strikethrough appears across that particular todo. When you reload the browser, you can see that the changes made to the todo list persist.

Let us take a brief recap of all that we have done:

- First, we created an Angular application using the Angular-CLI
- Then we created a server file, where we required our dependencies, created an express app, set our API routes, declared a port for our server to listen to, added parsers for post data, and so on
- We then defined our source of data which was a `.json` file of todos communicating with **diskdb**
- Created an Angular component
- Created a service with `get`, `post`, `put`, and `delete` methods that communicate with the REST API

Let us look at another example. We'll create a simple app to display a list of users together with their emails, and phone numbers. The users will also have a true or false state, indicating whether they are available or unavailable.

Build a user directory with Angular

The application we are about to build will have a REST API which will be created during the course of this example. In this simple example, we'll be creating a users app which will be quite simple. The app will basically be a table which contains a list of users together with their email addresses and phone numbers. Each user in the table will have an *active* state whose value is a boolean. We will be able to change the *active* state of a particular user from false to true and vice versa. The app will give us the ability to add new users and also delete users from the table. Just like the previous example, diskDB will be used as the database for this example. We will have an Angular service which contains methods that will be responsible for communicating with the REST end points. These methods will be responsible for making get, post, put, and delete requests to the REST API. The first method in the service will be responsible for making a get request to the API. This will enable us to retrieve all the users from the back end. Next, we will have another method that makes a post request to the API. This will enable us to add new users to the array of existing users.

The next method we shall have will be responsible for making a delete request to the API in order to enable the deletion of a user. Finally, we shall have a method that makes a put request to the API. This will be the method that gives us the ability to edit/modify the state of a user. In order to make these requests to the REST API, we will have to make use of the HttpModule. The aim of this section is to solidify your knowledge of HTTP. As a JavaScript and, in fact, an Angular developer, you are bound to make interactions with APIs and web servers almost all the time. So much data used by developers today is in form of APIs and in order to make interactions with these APIs, we need to constantly make use of HTTP requests. As a matter of fact, HTTP is the foundation of data communication for the web.

Create a new Angular app

As shown previously, to start a new Angular app, run the following command:

```
ng new user
```

This creates the Angular 2 user app.

Install the following dependencies:

- Express
- Body-parser
- Cors

```
npm install express body-parser cors --save
```

Create a Node server

Create a file called `server.js` at the root of the project directory. This will be our node server.

Populate `server.js` with the following block of code:

```
// Require dependencies
const express = require('express');
const path = require('path');
const http = require('http');
const cors = require('cors');
const bodyParser = require('body-parser');
// Get our API routes
const route = require('./route');
const app = express();
app.use(bodyParser.json());
app.use(bodyParser.urlencoded({ extended: false }));
// Use CORS
app.use(cors());
// Set our api routes
app.use('/api', route);
/**
* Get port from environment.
*/
const port = process.env.PORT || '3000';
/**
* Create HTTP server.
*/
const server = http.createServer(app);
//Listen on provided port
app.listen(port);
console.log('server is listening');
```

What's going on here is pretty simple:

- We required and made use of the dependencies
- We defined and set the API routes
- We set a port for our server to listen to

The API routes are being required from ./route, but this path does not exist yet. Let's quickly create it.

At the root of the project directory, create a file called route.js. This is where the API routes will be made. We need to have a form of a database from where we can fetch, post, delete, and modify data.

Just as in the previous example, we will make use of diskdb. The route will pretty much have the same pattern as in the first example.

Install diskDB

Run the following in the project folder to install diskdb:

```
npm install diskdb
```

Create a users.json file at the root of the project directory to serve as our database collection where we have our users' details.

Populate users.json with the following:

```
[{"name": "Marcel", "email": "test1@gmail.com", "phone_number":"08012345",
"isOnline":false}]
```

Now, update route.js.

```
route.js
const express = require('express');
const router = express.Router();
const db = require('diskdb');
db.connect(__dirname, ['users']);
//save
router.post('/users', function(req, res, next) {
var user = req.body;
if (!user.name && !(user.email + '') && !(user.phone_number + '') &&
!(user.isActive + '')) {
res.status(400);
res.json({
error: 'error'
```

```
});
} else {
console.log('ds');
db.users.save(todo);
res.json(todo);
}
});
//get
router.get('/users', function(req, res, next) {
var foundUsers = db.users.find();
console.log(foundUsers);
res.json(foundUsers);
foundUsers = db.users.find();
console.log(foundUsers);
});
//updateUsers
router.put('/user/:id', function(req, res, next) {
var updUser = req.body;
console.log(updUser, req.params.id)
db.users.update({_id: req.params.id}, updUser);
res.json({ msg: req.params.id + ' updated' });
});
//delete
router.delete('/user/:id', function(req, res, next) {
console.log(req.params);
db.users.remove({
_id: req.params.id
});
res.json({ msg: req.params.id + ' deleted' });
});
module.exports = router;
```

We've created a REST API with the API routes, using diskDB as the database.

Start the server using the following command:

```
node server.js
```

The server is running and it is listening to the assigned port. Now, open up the browser and go to http://localhost:3000/api/users.

Here, we can see the data that we imputed to the `users.json` file. This shows that our routes are working and we are getting data from the database.

Create a new component

Run the following command to create a new component:

```
ng g component user
```

This creates `user.component.ts`, `user.component.html`, `user.component.css` and `user.component.spec.ts` files. `User.component.spec.ts` is used for testing, therefore we will not be making use of it in this chapter. The newly created component is automatically imported into `app.module.ts`. We have to tell the root component about the user component. We'll do this by importing the selector from `user.component.ts` into the root template component (`app.component.html`):

```
<div style="text-align:center">
<app-user></app-user>
</div>
```

Create a service

The next step is to create a service that interacts with the API that we created earlier:

```
ng generate service user
```

This creates a user service called the `user.service.ts`. Next, import `UserService` class into `app.module.ts` and include it to the providers array:

```
Import rxjs/add/operator/map in the imports section.
import { Injectable } from '@angular/core';
import { Http, Headers } from '@angular/http';
import 'rxjs/add/operator/map';
Within the UserService class, define a constructor and pass in the angular
2 HTTP service.
import { Injectable } from '@angular/core';
import { Http, Headers } from '@angular/http';
import 'rxjs/add/operator/map';
@Injectable()
export class UserService {
constructor(private http: Http) {}
}
```

Within the service class, write a method that makes a `get` request to fetch all users and their details from the API:

```
getUser() {
return this.http
.get('http://localhost:3000/api/users')
.map(res => res.json());
}
```

Write the method that makes a `post` request and creates a new todo:

```
addUser(newUser) {
var headers = new Headers();
headers.append('Content-Type', 'application/json');
return this.http
.post('http://localhost:3000/api/user', JSON.stringify(newUser), {
headers: headers
})
.map(res => res.json());
}
```

Write another method that makes a `delete` request. This will enable us to delete a user from the collection of users:

```
deleteUser(id) {
return this.http
.delete('http://localhost:3000/api/user/' + id)
.map(res => res.json());
}
```

Finally, write a method that makes a `put` request. This method will enable us to modify the state of a user:

```
updateUser(user) {
var headers = new Headers();
headers.append('Content-Type', 'application/json');
return this.http
.put('http://localhost:3000/api/user/' + user._id, JSON.stringify(user), {
headers: headers
})
.map(res => res.json());
}
```

Update `app.module.ts` to import `HttpModule` and `FormsModule` and include them to the imports array:

```
import { HttpModule } from '@angular/http';
import { FormsModule } from '@angular/forms';
.....
imports: [
.....
HttpModule,
FormsModule
]
```

The next thing to do is to teach the user component to use the service:

```
Import UserService in user.component.ts.
import {UserService} from '../user.service';
Next, include the service class in the user component constructor.
constructor(private userService: UserService) { }.
Just below the exported UserComponent class, add the following properties
and define their data types:
users: any = [];
user: any;
name: any;
email: any;
phone_number: any;
isOnline: boolean;
```

Now, we can make use of the methods from the user service in the user component.

Updating user.component.ts

Within the `ngOnInit` method, make use of the user service to `get` all users from the API:

```
ngOnInit() {
this.userService.getUser().subscribe(users => {
console.log(users);
this.users = users;
});
}
```

Below the `ngOnInit` method, write a method that makes use of the `post` method in the user service to add new users:

```
addUser(event) {
event.preventDefault();
var newUser = {
name: this.name,
email: this.email,
phone_number: this.phone_number,
isOnline: false
};
this.userService.addUser(newUser).subscribe(user => {
this.users.push(user);
this.name = '';
this.email = '';
this.phone_number = '';
});
}
```

Let's make use of the `delete` method from the user service to enable us to delete users:

```
deleteUser(id) {
var users = this.users;
this.userService.deleteUser(id).subscribe(data => {
console.log(id);
const index = this.users.findIndex(user => user._id == id);
users.splice(index, 1)
});
}
```

Finally, we'll make use of user service to make `put` requests to the API:

```
updateUser(user) {
var _user = {
_id: user._id,
name: user.name,
email: user.email,
phone_number: user.phone_number,
isActive: !user.isActive
};
this.userService.updateUser(_user).subscribe(data => {
const index = this.users.findIndex(user => user._id == _user._id)
this.users[index] = _user;
});
}
```

We have all our communication with the API, service, and component. We have to update `user.component.html` in order to illustrate all that we have done in the browser.

We'll be making use of bootstrap for styling. So, we have to import the bootstrap CDN in `index.html`:

```
<!doctype html>
<html lang="en">
<head>
//bootstrap CDN
<link rel="stylesheet"
href="https://maxcdn.bootstrapcdn.com/bootstrap/4.0.0-beta/css/bootstrap.min.css" integrity="sha384-
/Y6pD6FV/Vv2HJnA6t+vslU6fwYXjCFtcEpHbNJ0lyAFsXTsjBbfaDjzALeQsN6M"
crossorigin="anonymous">
<meta charset="utf-8">
<title>User</title>
<base href="/">
<meta name="viewport" content="width=device-width, initial-scale=1">
<link rel="icon" type="image/x-icon" href="favicon.ico">
</head>
<body>
<app-root></app-root>
</body>
</html>
```

Updating user.component.html

Here is the component template for the user component:

```
<form class="form-inline" (submit) = "addUser($event)">
<div class="form-row">
<div class="col">
<input type="text" class="form-control" [(ngModel)] ="name" name="name">
</div>
<div class="col">
<input type="text" class="form-control" [(ngModel)] ="email" name="email">
</div>
<div class="col">
<input type="text" class="form-control" [(ngModel)] ="phone_number"
name="phone_number">
</div>
</div> <br>
<button class="btn btn-primary" type="submit" (click) =
"addUser($event)"><h4>Add User</h4></button>
</form>
```

```
<table class="table table-striped" >
<thead>
<tr>
<th>Name</th>
<th>Email</th>
<th>Phone_Number</th>
<th>Active</th>
</tr>
</thead>
<tbody *ngFor="let user of users">
<tr>
<td>{{user.name}}</td>
<td>{{user.email}}</td>
<td>{{user.phone_number}}</td>
<td>{{user.isActive}}</td>
<td><input type="submit" class="btn btn-warning" value="Update Status"
(click)="updateUser(user)" [ngStyle]="{ 'text-decoration-color:':
user.isActive ? 'blue' : ''}"></td>
<td><button (click) ="deleteUser(user._id)" class="btn btn-
danger">Delete</button></td>
</tr>
</tbody>
</table>
```

A lot is going on in the preceding code, let's drill down into the code block:

- We have a form which takes in three inputs and a submit button which triggers the `addUser()` method when clicked
- There is a **delete** button which triggers the `delete` method when it is clicked
- There is also an update status input element that triggers the `updateUser()` method when clicked
- We created a table in which our users' details will be displayed utilizing Angular's `*ngFor` directive and Angular's interpolation binding syntax, `{{}}`

Some extra styling will be added to the project. Go to `user.component.css` and add the following:

```
form{
margin-top: 20px;
margin-left: 20%;
size: 50px;
}
table{
margin-top:20px;
height: 50%;
width: 50%;
```

```
margin-left: 20%;
}
button{
margin-left: 20px;
}
```

Running the app

Open up two command line interfaces/terminals. In both of them, navigate to the project directory. Run node `server.js` to start the server in one. Run `ng serve` in the other to serve the Angular 2 app.

Open up the browser and go to `localhost:4200`.

In this simple users app, we can perform all CRUD operations. We can create new users, get users, delete users, and update the state of users.

By default, a newly added user's active state is false. That can be changed by clicking on the **change state** button.

Summary

Working with actual data from a database or from an API is quite important when developing any application. HTTP along with observables and Rxjs made it possible to work with the desired set of data from an API, and also perform all CRUD operations.

In the next chapter, we'll be taking a look at writing unit tests and debugging.

12
Testing and Debugging

Testing is crucial to building production-ready applications. In unit tests, we test a component independent of external sources to make sure it works as expected. Angular 2 has testing capabilities bundled with it out of the box. In this chapter, we will take a look at performing unit test on the following elements:

- Components
- Services
- Pipes
- Directives

Angular 2 testing tools

Some of the tools that aid testing in Angular 2 are as follows:

- Jasmine
- Karma
- Protractor
- Angular 2 testing platform

Let's take a deeper look at each one of them.

Jasmine

Jasmine is an open source testing framework. It uses behavior-driven notation that brings about improved testing.

Main concepts of Jasmine

Before we dig into so practical testing cases, here are some Jasmine concepts you should know:

- **Suites**: These are written in and described by the `describe` blocks. They appear in the form of functions.
- **Spec definitions**: `it (string, function)` functions. The body of this function holds the actual assertions.
- **Expectations**: These are assertions that evaluate to a Boolean value. This is used to see if an input is equal to the expected value.
- **Matchers**: These are helpers for common assertions, for example, `toB0` (expected), `toEqual` (expected).

Karma

Karma is a JavaScript test runner created by the Angular team. Karma can be a part of the continuous integration processes for a project as well as a part of its development.

Protractor

Protractor is an end-to-end test framework for Angular applications. With Protractor, you can set up expectations and test against our assumptions. As the name implies, end-to-end tests not only ensure that the system works by itself but also validates its functionality with external systems. They explore the application as the end user experiences it.

Angular testing platform

Angular testing platform is used to test the interaction of classes with Angular and the DOM. Angular testing platform gives us liberty to examine an instance of a class without any dependence on Angular or injected values.

In this chapter, we will be focusing on Jasmine and Karma for testing.

When a new project is created using Angular-CLI, the `e2e` folder containing the end-to-end tests using Protractor is also created, along with the `karma.conf.js` and `protractor.conf.js` files, which are the configuration files for Karma and Protractor tests.

Using Karma (with Jasmine)

With Karma, you can test your code while running your application because Karma creates a browser environment for testing. Besides your browser, you can also test your code in other devices, such as phones and tablets.

Jasmine is a behavior-driven development framework for testing the JavaScript code. Being dependency free, Jasmine doesn't require a DOM and is often used together with Karma. We will now proceed to create a new project and test its elements.

Creating a new project

We will create a new project named `Angular-test` with the following command:

```
ng new Angular-test
```

Installing the Karma CLI

To install the Karma CLI, enter the following command:

```
npm install -g karma-cli
```

Our test will be executed in a `.spec.ts` file. Create a new test file (`sampletest.spec.ts`) in the `./app/` folder and copy the following:

```
// ./app/sampletest.spec.ts
describe('Sample Test', () => {
 it('true is true', () => expect(true).toBe(true));
 });

 import {AppComponent} from './app.component';

 describe('AppComponent', () => {
 beforeEach(function() {
 this.app = new AppComponent();
 });

 it('should have hello property', function() {
 expect(this.app.hello).toBe('Hello, World!');
 });
 });
```

In the preceding code, we first write a sample test to showcase the main concepts in Jamine. We create a test suite, define our test suite, and write the expectations. In the sample test, we do a simple check to see that `true` is the same as `true`.

We also write a simple test for `AppComponent`. We expect the component to have a `hello` property that is equal to `Hello, World`. Let's ensure that the test passes by updating `app.component.ts`:

```
private hello: string = 'Hello, World!';
```

We have satisfied Karma's configuration by creating the file with the `.spec.ts` extension.

You can test several components as well. For example, when you create new components through Angular CLI, it automatically creates the test files (`.spec.ts`) for the components, which do nothing but test whether the components are working correctly together with the other components. For Angular, the convention is to have a `.spec.ts` file for each `.ts` file. The files are run using the Jasmine JavaScript test framework through the Karma task runner when you use the `ng test` command.

Configuring Karma

In order to configure our Karma, we need to update the `karma.conf.js` file. The default one has the following content:

```
// ./karma.conf.js.
module.exports = function (config) {
 config.set({
 basePath: '',
 frameworks: ['jasmine', 'angular-cli'],
 plugins: [
 require('karma-jasmine'),
 require('karma-chrome-launcher'),
 require('karma-remap-istanbul'),
 require('angular-cli/plugins/karma')
 ],
 files: [
 { pattern: './src/test.ts', watched: false }
 ],
 preprocessors: {
 './src/test.ts': ['angular-cli']
 },
 remapIstanbulReporter: {
 reports: {
 html: 'coverage',
```

```
lcovonly: './coverage/coverage.lcov'
}
},
angularCli: {
config: './angular-cli.json',
environment: 'dev'
},
reporters: ['progress', 'karma-remap-istanbul'],
port: 9876,
colors: true,
logLevel: config.LOG_INFO,
autoWatch: true,
browsers: ['PhantomJS'],
singleRun: false
});
};
```

Here, we are showing that the PhantomJS browser will be used; Jasmine testing framework and Webpack will be used for bundling the files.

Testing the components

Components are the centerpiece of Angular. They are the nucleus around which the rest of the framework is built. We'll explore what a component is, why it is important, and how to test it.

Our testing strategy revolves around verifying the correctness of the properties and methods of the classes that make up the components.

When writing unit tests for components, we initialize the component and inject any dependencies manually rather than bootstrapping the application.

The TestBed function will be used for testing the component, which is the main entry to all of Angular's testing interface. It will enable us to create our components for use in running unit tests.

TestBed is the primary API for writing unit tests for Angular applications and libraries.

Create a new component named sample:

```
ng generate component sample
```

This automatically generates the `.ts` and `.spec.ts` files. We will also add some tests to the generated `.spec.ts` file to get a hang of how the testing works:

```
//sample.component.ts
import { Component, OnInit } from '@angular/core';

@Component({
selector: 'app-sample',
templateUrl: './sample.component.html',
styleUrls: ['./sample.component.css']
})
export class SampleComponent implements OnInit {
title = 'Test Sample Component';
constructor() { }
ngOnInit() {
}
}
```

Here is the updated test spec:

```
//sample.component.spec.ts
import { ComponentFixture, TestBed } from '@angular/core/testing';
import { By } from '@angular/platform-browser';
import { DebugElement } from '@angular/core';
import { SampleComponent } from './sample.component';
describe('SampleComponent (inline template)', () => {
let component: SampleComponent;
let fixture: ComponentFixture<SampleComponent>;
// For Debugging HTML Elements
let debug: DebugElement;
let htmlElem: HTMLElement;
beforeEach(() => {
TestBed.configureTestingModule({
declarations: [ SampleComponent ], // Our Test sample component
});
// Get the ComponentFixture
fixture = TestBed.createComponent(SampleComponent);
component = fixture.componentInstance; // SampleComponent test instance
// CSS Element selector
debug = fixture.debugElement.query(By.css('h1'));
htmlElem = debug.nativeElement;
});
it('don't show any title on DOM until we call `detectChanges`', () => {
expect(htmlElem.textContent).toEqual('');
});
it('should display original title', () => {
fixture.detectChanges();
expect(htmlElem.textContent).toContain(component.title);
```

```
});
it('should display a different test title', () => {
component.title = Different Test Title';
fixture.detectChanges();
expect(htmlElem.textContent).toContain('Different Test Title');
});
});
```

The `createComponent` method in `TestBed` creates an instance of the component. These tests tell Angular when to perform change detection through `fixture.detectChanges()` (which we received from `createComponent`). `TestBed.createComponent`, by default, doesn't trigger the change detection. This is why specific parts in our test won't show the changes on the DOM.

Making use of `ComponentFixtureAutoDetect` from `@angular/core/testing` enables you to apply auto detection globally:

```
TestBed.configureTestingModule({
  declarations: [ SampleComponent ],
  providers: [
  { provide: ComponentFixtureAutoDetect, useValue: true }
  ]
  })
```

Testing services

Let's create a sample service. Our service has only one method that returns an array of the available users for the application:

```
//a simple service
export class UsersService {
get() {
return ['Ken', 'Mark', 'Chris'];
}
}
```

We instantiate the service using the `beforeEach` method. This is a good practice even if we only have one spec. We are checking each individual user and the total count:

```
describe('Service: UsersService', () => {
let service;
beforeEach(() => TestBed.configureTestingModule({
providers: [ UsersService ]
}));
beforeEach(inject([UsersService], s => {
```

```
service = s;
}));
it('should return available users', () => {
let users = service.get();
expect(users).toContain('en');
expect(users).toContain('es');
expect(users).toContain('fr');
expect(users.length).toEqual(3);
});
});
```

Testing using HTTP

Let's start by creating a `users.serviceHttp.ts` file:

```
// users.serviceHttp.ts
export class UsersServiceHttp {
constructor(private http:Http) { }
get(){
return this.http.get('api/users.json')
.map(response => response.json());
}
}
```

In this case it uses `http.get()` to fetch the data from a JSON file. We then used `Observable.map()` to transform the response into the final result using `json()`.

The difference that exists between this test and the previous one is the use of an asynchronous test:

```
//users.serviceHttp.spec.ts
describe('Service: UsersServiceHttp', () => {
let service;
//setup
beforeEach(() => TestBed.configureTestingModule({
imports: [ HttpModule ],
providers: [ UsersServiceHttp ]
}));
beforeEach(inject([UsersServiceHttp], s => {
service = s;
}));
//specs
it('should return available users', async(() => {
service.get().subscribe(x => {
expect(x).toContain('en');
expect(x).toContain('es');
```

```
expect(x).toContain('fr');
expect(x.length).toEqual(3);
});
}));
})
```

Testing using MockBackend

A more sensible approach is to replace HTTP calls with a MockBackend. For doing this, we can use the beforeEach() method. This will allow us to mock our responses and avoid hitting the real backend, thereby boosting our tests:

```
//users.serviceHttp.spec.ts
describe('MockBackend: UsersServiceHttp', () => {
let mockbackend, service;
//setup
beforeEach(() => {
TestBed.configureTestingModule({
imports: [ HttpModule ],
providers: [
UsersServiceHttp,
{ provide: XHRBackend, useClass: MockBackend }
]
})
});
beforeEach(inject([UsersServiceHttp, XHRBackend], (_service, _mockbackend)
=> {
service = _service;
mockbackend = _mockbackend;
}));
//specs
it('should return mocked response (sync)', () => {
  let response = ["ru", "es"];
  mockbackend.connections.subscribe(connection => {
    connection.mockRespond(new Response(new ResponseOptions({
     body: JSON.stringify(response)
    })));
    service.get().subscribe(users => {
     expect(users).toContain('ru');
     expect(users).toContain('es');
     expect(users.length).toBe(2);
    });
  });
});
```

We made our mocked response. So, when we finally make the call to our service, it gets the expected results.

Testing a directive

The directive decorator in Angular is used to decorate a class that has the responsibility of extending components in the DOM, based on the defined methods and logic.

Take this directive that changes the background, for example:

```
import { Directive, HostBinding, HostListener } from '@angular/core';

@Directive({
  selector: '[appBackgroundChanger]'
})
export class BackgroundChangerDirective {

  @HostBinding('style.background-color') backgroundColor: string;

  @HostListener('mouseover') onHover() {
    this.backgroundColor = 'red';
  }

  @HostListener('mouseout') onLeave() {
    this.backgroundColor = 'inherit';
  }

}
```

We will be making use of an attribute directive, `logClicks`, which logs the number of clicks on the host element.

Let's create a `container` component. This will be our host, reproducing the events emitted by our directive:

```
@Component({
  selector: 'container',
  template: `<div log-clicks (changes)="changed($event)"></div>`,
  directives: [logClicks]
})
export class Container {
@Output() changes = new EventEmitter();
changed(value){
this.changes.emit(value);
}
}
```

Here is the test spec:

```
describe('Directive: logClicks', () => {
let fixture;
let container;
let element;
//setup
beforeEach(() => {
TestBed.configureTestingModule({
declarations: [ Container, logClicks ]
});
fixture = TestBed.createComponent(Container);
container = fixture.componentInstance; // to access properties and methods
element = fixture.nativeElement; // to access DOM element
});
//specs
it('should increment counter', fakeAsync(() => {
let div = element.querySelector('div');
//set up subscriber
container.changes.subscribe(x => {
expect(x).toBe(1);
});
//trigger click on container
div.click();
//execute all pending asynchronous calls
tick();
}));
})
```

The `beforeEach` method is used to separate the logic for creating the component from the tests. DOM API is recommended and is used to trigger the click on the container.

Testing a pipe

Pipes in Angular are functions that can transform input data into a user-readable format. Here is an example of a custom pipe called `capitalise` in our `src` folder, using the standard `String.toUpperCase()`. This is just an example; Angular already has its own pipe for capitalization:

```
//capitalise.pipe.ts
import {Pipe, PipeTransform} from '@angular/core';
@Pipe({
name: 'capitalise'
})
export class CapitalisePipe implements PipeTransform {
transform(value: string): string {
```

```
if (typeof value !== 'string') {
throw new Error('Requires a String as input');
}
return value.toUpperCase();
}
}
```

The `capitalise.pipe.spec.ts` file will be as follows:

```
describe('Pipe: CapitalisePipe', () => {
let pipe;
//setup
beforeEach(() => TestBed.configureTestingModule({
providers: [ CapitalisePipe ]
}));
beforeEach(inject([CapitalisePipe], p => {
pipe = p;
}));
//specs
it('should work with empty string', () => {
expect(pipe.transform('')).toEqual('');
});
it('should capitalise', () => {
expect(pipe.transform('wow')).toEqual('WOW');
});
it('should throw with invalid values', () => {
//must use arrow function for expect to capture exception
expect(()=>pipe.transform(undefined)).toThrow();
expect(()=>pipe.transform()).toThrow();
expect(()=>pipe.transform()).toThrowError('Requires a String as input');
});
})
```

Debugging

Augury is a Chrome extension for debugging Angular applications, just like Batarang was used for debugging Angular 1 apps. Once installed, the extension is seen as a dev tool plugin that has features for testing out your Angular app's behavior.

Augury

Augury inspects and visualizes the component tree with different properties of one or more components. Install the Augury tools from the Augury Chrome extension page, (`https://chrome.google.com/webstore/detail/augury/elgalmkoelokbchhkhacckoklkejnhcd`) **and click on the ADD TO CHROME button. Once the installation is completed, the following steps need to be taken in order to work with Augury:**

- Use *Ctrl* + *Shift* + *I* to open the Chrome Developer Tools window.
- Click on Augury to open the tool. It displays menu options such as **Component Tree**, **Router Tree**, and **NgModules**.

The Augury icon can be seen in the top-right corner of your browser once it is installed.

Open it and you will see a list of currently loaded components in your application, sorted by their hierarchy. You can also see where they are located in the DOM. Any change made to a component will also be shown.

With this, it becomes easier for developers to get an insight on how their apps are performing and where the problems and bugs could be originating from:

Augury features

Let's look at some of the Augury features in detail.

Component tree

This is the first view that is visible, which shows the loaded components belonging to the application:

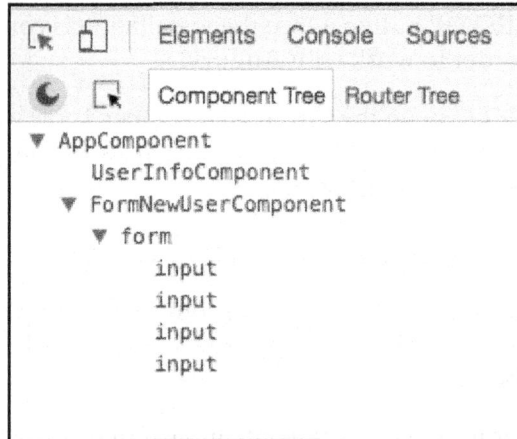

The component tree displays a hierarchical relationship of the components. More information about a component can also be shown by selecting each component:

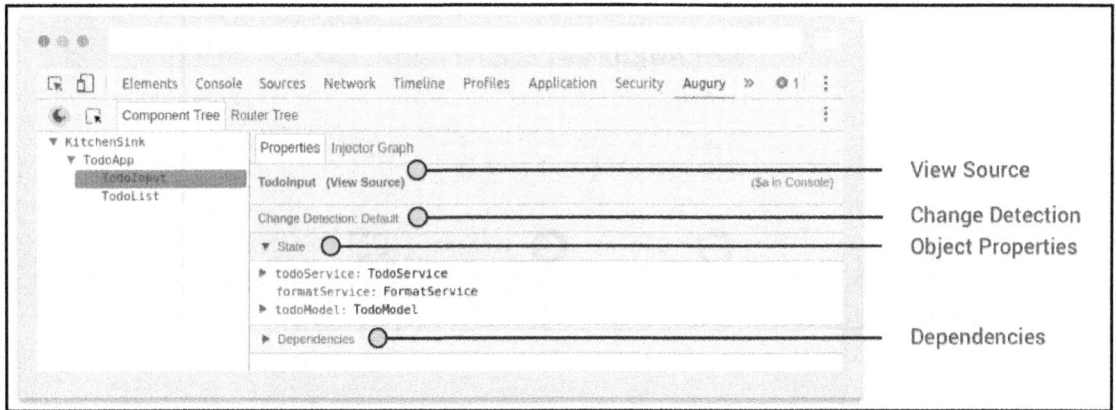

Router tree

The router tree displays information on how every component in your application tree is routed. It does this in a hierarchical order:

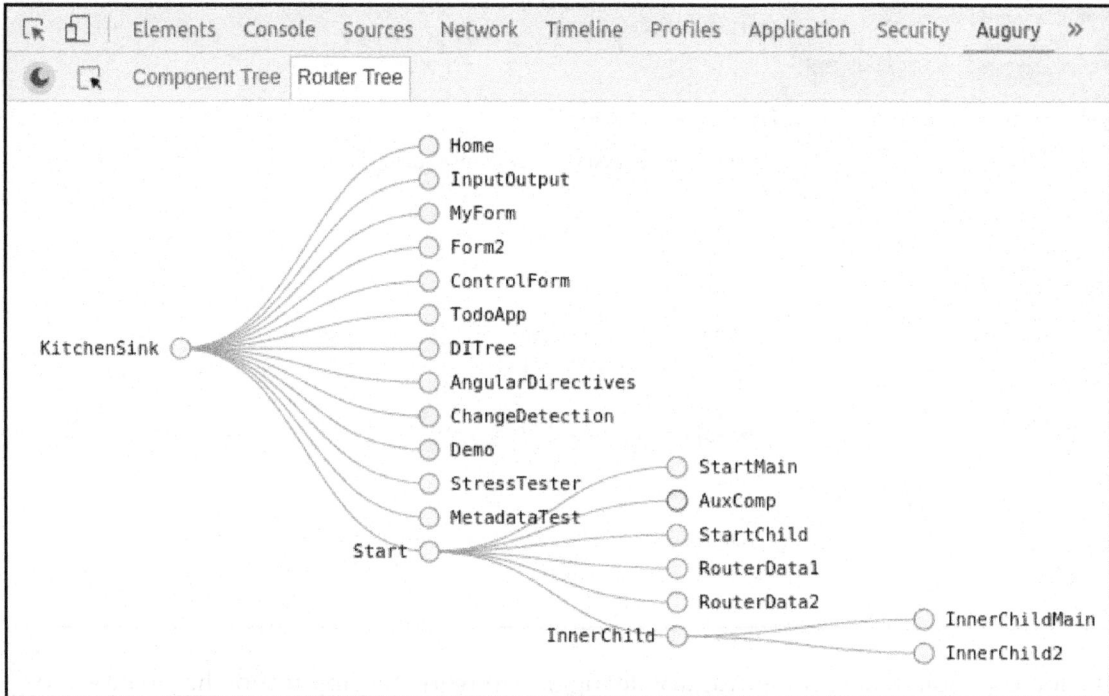

Source map

It is noteworthy that the TypeScript code will show whether a source map file exists. In production, if no source map is found, only the compiled JavaScript code will be displayed, which may also be minified and difficult to read.

Clicking on **Inject Graph** will display the dependency of components and services:

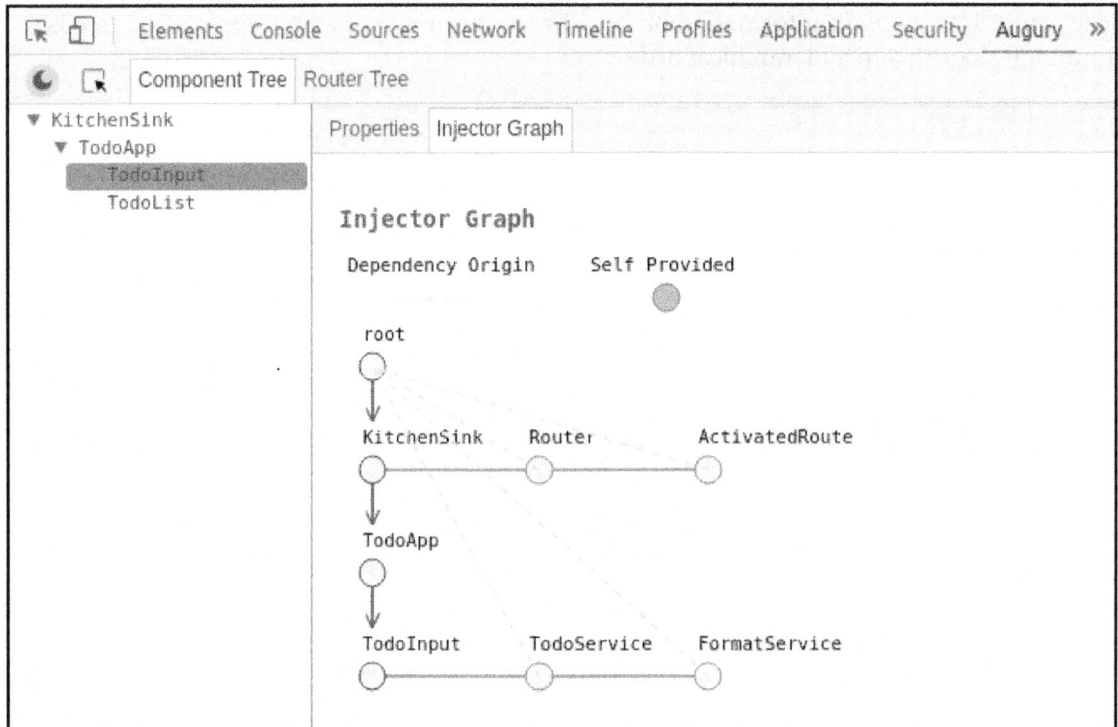

It should be noted that for the Augury debugging to work, the application has to be set to the development mode.

Summary

It is important to do unit tests because they run faster and we'll be able to get feedback faster. A good advantage of testing is that it helps against regressions (the changes that break existing code).

Debugging helps us identify and remove errors from our code. With Augury, developers can have visuals of the application through component trees and visual debugging tools. This makes debugging easier.

Index

Lightning Source UK Ltd.
Milton Keynes UK
UKOW07f2326141217
314491UK00004B/357/P

9 781786 460554